RIVER, COAST & CREEK

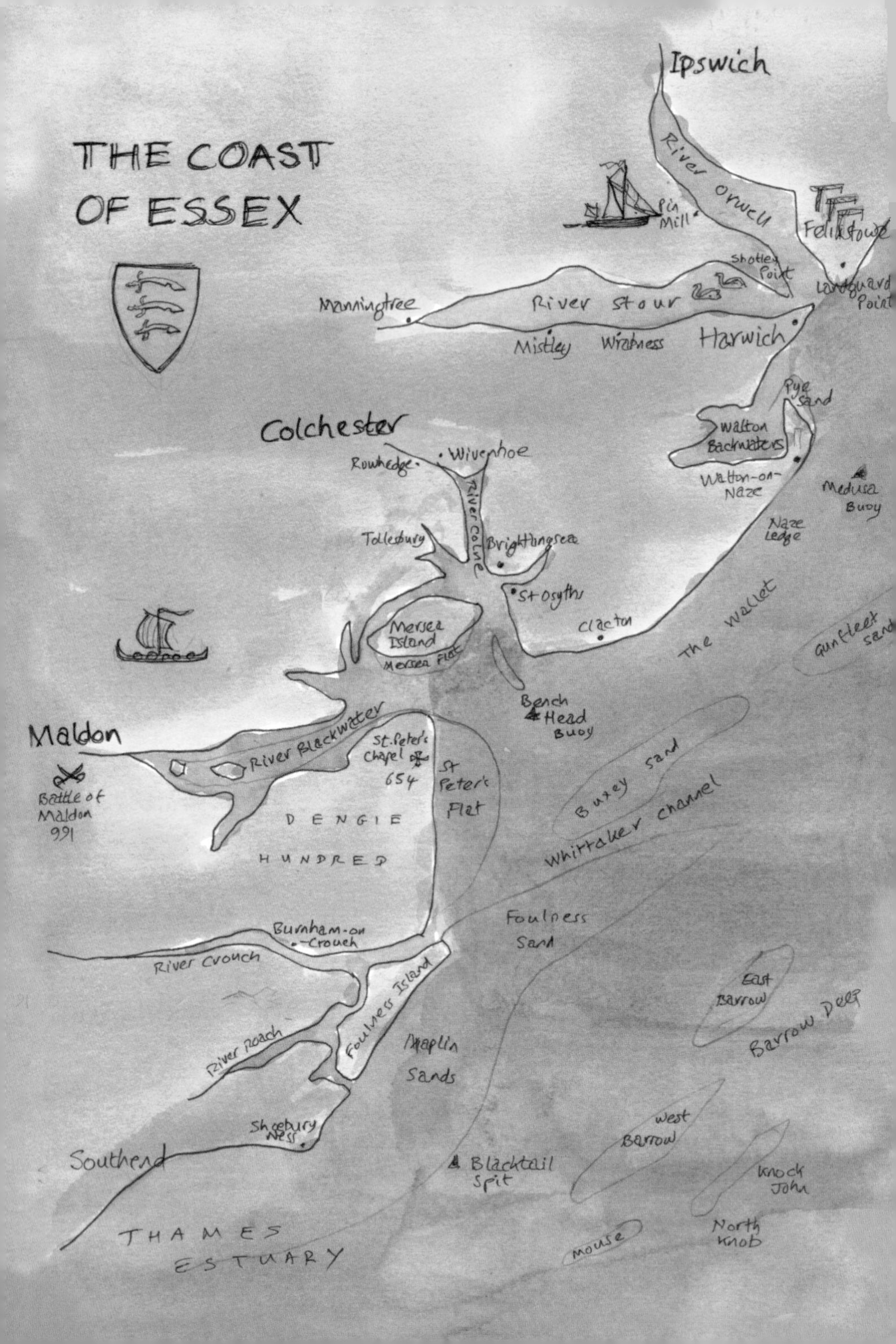

THE COAST OF ESSEX
Ipswich
River Orwell
Pin Mill
Felixstowe
Shotley Point
Landguard Point
Manningtree
River Stour
Mistley
Wrabness
Harwich
Pye Sand
Walton Backwaters
Walton-on-Naze
Medusa Buoy
Naze Ledge
Colchester
Rowhedge
Wivenhoe
River Colne
Tollesbury
Brightlingsea
St Osyths
Clacton
The Wallet
Gunfleet Sand
Mersea Island
Mersea Flat
Bench Head Buoy
Maldon
River Blackwater
St. Peter's Chapel 654
St Peter's Flat
Battle of Maldon 991
DENGIE HUNDRED
Buxey Sand
Whittaker Channel
Foulness Sand
Burnham-on-Crouch
River Crouch
Foulness Island
East Barrow
Barrow Deep
River Roach
Maplin Sands
Shoebury Ness
Southend
Blacktail Spit
West Barrow
Knock John
North Knob
Mouse
THAMES ESTUARY

Judith Ellis

RIVER, COAST & CREEK

An Exploration of Maritime Essex

with illustrations by the author

and a few red herrings

By the same author

TWO POINTS EAST
A View of Maritime Norfolk

CURLEW COAST
Diversions on Maritime Suffolk

THE RED HERRING
BOOK OF FOOD FACTS

Published by Red Herring Publishing

Designed by **studio medlikova**
Edited by Charlie Watson

ISBN 978-1-9997839-5-2

A CIP record for this book is available from the British Library

Printed and bound in the UK by Swallowtail Print Ltd, Norwich.

In memory of Angela and Ian Houston, whose friendship and generosity first brought me to this coast, and of the many happy hours shared aboard the Thames sailing barge *Raybel.*

CONTENTS

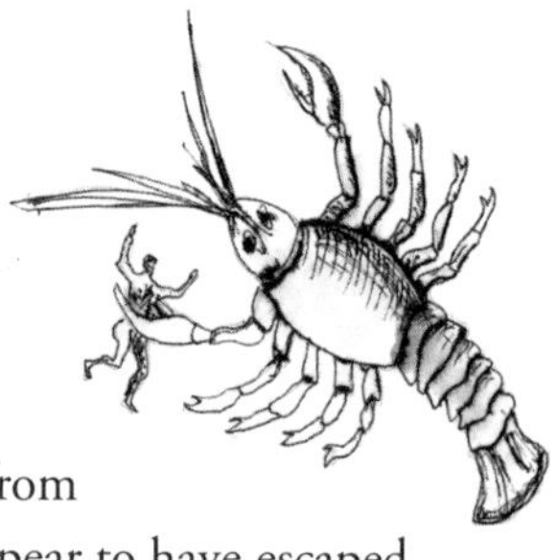

The drawings of sea monsters have all been taken from
existing medieval maps and one or two of them appear to have escaped.

It is one of the last wild places of England, a low far-reaching expanse of grass and reed and half-submerged meadowlands ending in the great saltings and mud flats and tidal pools near the restless sea.

Tidal creeks and estuaries and the crooked, meandering arms of many little rivers whose mouths lap at the edge of the ocean cut through the sodden land that seems to rise and fall and breathe with the recurrence of the daily tides.

Paul Gallico, from *The Snow Goose*

INTRODUCTION

I first came to Essex by sea. We had left Pin Mill earlier that morning, with the air of anticipation that always accompanies the slipping of a mooring, the filling of a sail and the insistent hissing of a kettle on the hob below. Except on a Thames sailing barge, 'slipping a mooring' is a hardly the right description for the twenty minutes of hard grind on the anchor-winch which Angela and I had put in earlier, the steady click of the ratchet ringing across the water as we slowly wound in the long, heavy chain which had secured us for the last few days to the muddy bottom of Butterman's Bay, a small bay within hailing distance of the hard at Pin Mill.

I had little idea then that I would return to this coast many times over the next thirty or so years, and that its magic would never fail to enchant me.

When the early Saxon settlers first came here in the centuries following the departure of the Romans, they would have found a landscape familiar to them. A coast of saltmarsh, mud and rivers with a myriad of channels, creeks and inlets. They would have recognised the rich pickings to be had here, with fish and oysters aplenty and wildfowl to be hunted in the marshes. They were not to know that in time they would give their name to this part of Britain, which would become known as the land of the East Saxons and eventually Essex; and that subsequently, when all the east of Britain came under the Danelaw, a future generation of Anglo-Saxons would eventually drive out the occupying Danes, uniting the whole of England for the first time under their great king, Athelstan. But for the Saxon settlers, that was way into the future.

The coast of Suffolk has sand and shingle beaches and a number of small coastal towns, but the coast of Essex is very different: a glance at the map will show its relative inaccessability. Walton, Clacton and Southend are seaside resorts, but the rest of the coastal strip has very few roads and large areas are shown devoid of any marks at all other than a few dykes and creeks. It is largely vast flat areas of saltmarsh and mud, where the tide can go out a long way. Your map will show a definite demarcation between the sea and the land, but in reality where actually is the edge? At low tide it can be a very long way from its position at high water. Look more closely at the map and you will observe a seemingly infinite number of small creeks and inlets; if you stretched this part of the coast out until it was straight it would go on for ever. Essex has a great deal of liminal space – neither land nor sea – made up of saltings, water and mudflats. It is elemental and timeless. It was this space that ancient people thought was a transitional place between this world and another. Here they buried their dead and built sacred wood circles such as the 'sea henge' which was uncovered at low tide at Holme-next-the-Sea in Norfolk in 1998.

To hear the cry of the Essex coast you can do no better than to read the opening pages of Paul Gallico's *The Snow Goose*, where he captures the remoteness of these marshlands in hauntingly beautiful prose. It is the sheer extent of liminal area on this coast that I think gives it this air of otherworldliness, of mystery, some feeling that you can't quite put your finger on.

The story of East Anglia's coast is interesting in that geologically it is Britain's youngest coast. The North Sea as we know it now only appeared 10,000 or so years ago. Until then Britain was part of mainland Europe and the river Thames was part of the Rhine. As the last glacier retreated north, the land between Europe and its westernmost peninsula that would become Britain began to flood, gradually forming the North Sea. This accelerated in 6100 BC, when a great tsunami swept down this coast. A piece of the seabed shelf off the Norwegian coast suddenly slipped and a thirty-foot wall of water, hundreds of miles long, raced south. Britain was cut loose from the rest of Europe and was now an island which could only be reached by water.

This newly appeared east coast must also have been the place where early man first arrived from Europe in the long-distant past. Human footprints on the shore were exposed at Happisburgh in Norfolk after an exceptionally low tide in 2013. They were dated by examining pollen sediments in the mud and were found to be about 900,000 years old. Human remains have yet to be found here, but these footprints are thought to have been made by *Homo antecessor,* an early predecessor of our own species, *Homo sapiens.*

The youngest coast with the oldest history.

Moving forward now to the medieval period, trade up and down the coast and across the North Sea, or German Ocean as it was called then, was thriving. The flat-bottomed ships with a single sail, the *cogs,* favoured by the merchants of the Hansa, were once a common sight up and down the coast. But as the coastline starts to tuck in below Harwich and become part of the Thames Estuary, it also becomes less favourable for visiting ships, which have to pick their way through the many sandbanks and shallow channels to reach a port. As a result this part of the coast tended to look more towards the Thames Estuary and to France for trade, than to the ports of northern Europe and Scandinavia that were favoured by the merchants of Suffolk and Norfolk.

Exploring the maritime history of the East Anglian coast has become a fascinating journey for me. It began in King's Lynn, when a few days spent sketching led me to discover the rich past of the east coast, often forgotten now as so many coastal towns have suffered economically. It is the saddest thing to see a town struggling to maintain any life, having forgotten what it once was: its quayside thronged with ships from Europe, its boatyards busy building and repairing vessels; the sailmakers, the blacksmiths and the rope-makers; the fishing smacks and the smoke-houses curing fish; the air ringing with the sound of hammers, saws and the shouts of visiting sailors speaking

Dutch or French; the smell of tar on the air and the tang of fish. It is a world long lost to us.

So come with me on a journey charting the fortunes of this coast, from those early Anglo-Saxons through medieval times – when it was often safer to travel by sea than by land – to the fascinating evolution of sailing ships and all associated with them, until eventually the coming of the railway heralded the end of the great days of sail.

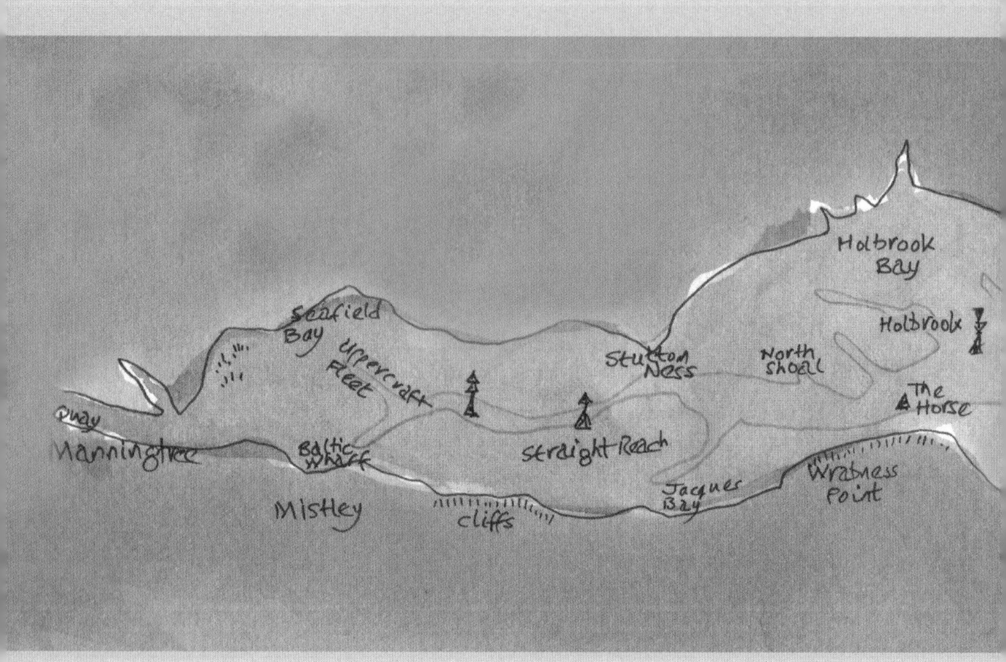
Holbrook Bay
Seafield Bay
Uppercraft Fleet
Stutton Ness
North Shoal
Holbrook
The Horse
Quay
Manningtree
Baltic Wharf
Straight Reach
Jacques Bay
Wrabness Point
Mistley
cliffs

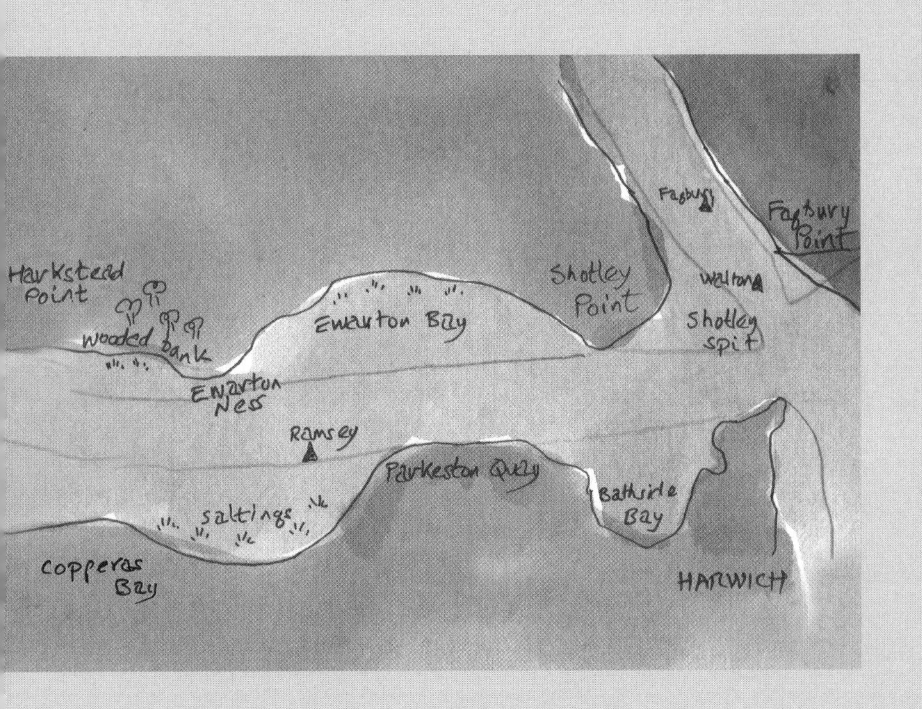

THE RIVER STOUR

THE RIVER STOUR

The land-based world divides itself politically. Often using rivers as boundaries, it has over the centuries divided itself into manors and liberties, hundreds and hides, parishes, shires and counties. But the maritime world has its own distinctive geography. Its features are estuaries, rivers and creeks; channels, sandbanks and shoals; high points or landmarks on the coast; and navigation marks that can range from just a few withies planted by local fishermen in the mud to the modern system of buoyage. It has its own language to describe this world: nesses and spits, neap tides and spring tides; sands and swatchways. Even a map is no longer a map but a chart.

A river may be somebody's boundary, but it is really about itself, an entity in its own right, not belonging to the land in any sense. The river in this context is a paradox, and the maritime world and the land-based one, existing side by side, are like parallel universes. One is part of the other, but not quite.

The river Stour marks the boundary between Suffolk and Essex, thus Felixstowe is in Suffolk but Harwich, just across the water, lies in Essex. The river is oblivious of this arbitrary boundary, though, and continues to flow eastward towards the sea: Harwich and Felixstowe, its twin ports, belong to the river not the land. As the train pulls out of Manningtree on the journey to London, it lifts the spirits to see, all too briefly, the broad, shining expanse of water as the Stour opens out before joining the Orwell on its way to the sea. You have had a glimpse into a world of sail, ships and shore-birds; a passing glance into a different world as the train hurtles on its way, leaving a fleeting impression of another way of living, in another time.

I have always loved rivers. A river is forever going somewhere, inviting you to join in on its journey; and should you be tempted, if you should step into a small boat (which are usually the most fun) it will go on enticing you to go a little further – just round the next bend, maybe just the next reach. Forever urging you on, it bewitches and enchants. Each straight part of a river is called a reach, and local users of the river will still remember some of their names. These names sometimes reflect the hazards of navigation, a common name being Troublesome Reach, flagging up the vagaries of the wind flow altered by nearby trees, buildings or hills, or maybe the river is too narrow or not deep enough for ease of sail. Sometimes the names are an echo of a farmstead long disappeared, a barge skipper, a local resident or some long-forgotten incident, leaving nothing behind now but a name on a map. The rivers of the east coast are generally slower in motion than their faster flowing brethren in more hilly parts of the country. Here the land lies gently and a river has time to amble at a more leisurely pace towards saltmarsh and mudflat.

In the distant past a village would up grow on the banks of a river, for besides providing water it would be a source of food and transport. The network of rivers made a natural infrastructure for communication. Goods and gossip would travel up and down a river's course, men would fish and catch wildfowl for the table, boys would search for birds' eggs among the reeds, women would bring the washing down to its banks, and reed-cutters would harvest reeds for the thatching of roofs and sedges for the capping.

Watermills would be built to grind grain and boatyards established to build the smaller vessels needed for river transport – punts, rowing skiffs, wherries, barges and lighters. All life passed along a river.

The villages of Lawford, Manningtree and Mistley seem to have now merged into one, starting at the head of the Stour estuary and straggling a little way down its southern bank. If you walk at high tide along the tree-lined bank, known as Mistley Walls, with a fresh easterly breeze sending little waves up the sunlit water, it appears to be a sizeable river. But return at low tide and what you will see is acres of mud with just a narrow deepwater channel winding its way up to Manningtree. A river this shallow was never going to be able sustain enough shipping to develop as a major port, and Manningtree and Mistley had to be content with the few small trading ships and barges that were able to make the passage up to the quays to discharge their cargo and take on the grain and malt that was produced in this part of the country. The river above Manningtree, made famous by the paintings of John Constable, was dredged to allow horse-drawn barges to take grain from the farms down to the quays where it would be transferred to the waiting larger boats.

Mistley was quietly getting on with its life, serving the locality with its small port and building a few ships for the Royal Navy, when Richard Rigby decided to shake things up. Rigby's father and grandfather had made the family fortune as drapers in London, holding various colonial offices and making successful speculations during the great expansion of the British Empire. Living in the family home of Mistley Hall, Richard went into politics and acquired a fortune of his own in the eighteenth century, always preferring a safe and lucrative sinecure over promotion to more important roles. He did accept the role of Paymaster to the Forces, though, a well-paid post which he held for sixteen years, and he decided to spend some of his wealth on turning his home town of Mistley into a fashionable resort. He set to building new quays and commissioned Robert Adams, the go-to architect of the time, to build a new church and a saltwater bathing pool by the river.

For a brief period Mistleythorne, as it was known then, enjoyed a period of prosperity, but things began to go wrong when Richard fell from grace, losing his position as Paymaster. The bathing pool was never built, and the unusual church designed by Adams was demolished, except for its two towers, which stand rather oddly, side by side on the green, greeting your arrival to Mistley.

The extensive quays now lie mostly disused and the river is left to yachtsmen and the shelduck, swans and wading birds.

WALTON

Known now largely for its tower and sandy beaches, Walton once stood nine miles from the coast, a measure of just how much land the sea has taken over the centuries. The erosion is continuing at a rate of one or two metres a year and the whole area has been designated as a site of special scientific interest, or SSSI, for its geological significance, its habitat and the birds that breed and winter among the marshes.

Lacking the grandeur of the rocky coasts of Dorset and the west of the country, this is none the less an area of unique geological importance. The reason is the fossil-rich Red Crag formation which outcrops here. Composed of shells, sands and gravels, it was laid down under the sea 2.5 million years ago, when the climate was sub-tropical and large mammals roamed the land. Its red colour comes from oxidation of the iron pyrites found in the layer beneath. Rivers washed plant and animal material down into the sea, and fossilised twigs, pollens and shells can all be found here, the bivalve shells jutting out from the soft red cliffs.

The Naze Tower was built by Trinity House in 1720 as a navigation mark for the entrance to the Stour, Orwell and Hamford Water. It is octagonal in structure and originally had a beacon on top, which was replaced by a reflective light in the nineteenth century.

Exposed Red Crag is unique to this part of the world, only found on this stretch of the coast and into the southern part of the Suffolk coast. If you walk along the Crag Path and look up at the cliffs under the tower, you can see the different geological layers clearly. Forming the base layer is the impermeable, grey London clay, laid down 55 million years ago. The Junction Bed lies on top of this, forming a relatively deep layer between the clay and the overlying crag. It is from this junction layer that sharks' teeth are often washed out, to be found later on the beach at low tide. The beach is particularly famous for the teeth of *Carcharodon megalodon* – the largest shark ever to have lived – which can each be the size of a human hand, giving an estimated whole-shark size of around ten metres, about the size of a modern Orca whale, although some even larger teeth have been found which would give a shark length of a staggering eighteen metres.

The top, crag, layer is brickearth, otherwise known as loess, which is a sediment laid down from particles borne on the wind from wind erosion, thus indicating it was formed in between inundations with water.

Crags *are the sands, shells and gravels laid down on top of London clay and are subdivided into Coraline, Red, Norwich and Wroxham Crags, with Coraline the most recent and Wroxham the oldest. Crags are unique to Britain and were laid down 2.5 million years ago, making them Britain's youngest rocks.*

There was an elusive perfume on the air as I set off to walk the cliff path from the Naze Tower to Hamford Water, strange yet at the same time familiar. The path was lined with bramble bushes and the heat of the sun was sending out the scent of ripe blackberries, which mingled confusingly with the tang of iodine from the sea. Summer was moving into autumn, the swallows had departed and the flocks of incoming migrant birds were yet to appear. The Naze is a well-known viewpoint to observe migrating birds, and a man sitting on his electric scooter by the path, a pair of binoculars around his neck, told me that he had seen ospreys and flocks of redstarts from here. He said a pair of peregrines had nested under the Orwell Bridge last year.

Hamford Water, known on the nautical charts as Walton Backwaters, is the setting for *Secret Water*, one of Arthur Ransome's best-loved books. It tells the story of the Walker children (the Swallows) and Nancy and Peggy (the Amazons) camping on Horsey Island for a week to survey the Backwaters and complete a map which Commander Walker had started for them. I had last visited the place by Thames sailing barge nearly forty years ago. Navigable only by small boat around high water, when various small islands become apparent, the whole area dries out to that east coast speciality of sticky mud and marsh, revealing a maze of muddy creeks weaving through the saltings.

The 1971 film of The Snow Goose, *starring Richard Harris and Jenny Agutter, was filmed in Hamford Water*

It was the wreck of the *Deutschland*, a German passenger steamship, on the Kentish Knock sandbank in 1876 with the loss of fifty-seven lives, which led the RNLI to finally decide that Essex needed a lifeboat. This was funded by the drama section of the Honourable Artillery Company, which regularly held summer camps on the Naze. The lifeboat which bore their name was built by Forrest and Son at Limehouse Quay, Wivenhoe, for the sum of £394 10s and was one of the new thirty-seven-foot self-righting, pulling and sailing boats. Both the lifeboat house and its lifeboat were completed eight years later in 1884 and she went on to save eighty-four lives during her service, before being replaced by the *James Stevens No14* in 1900.

The Old LIfeboat House

James Stevens was a wealthy businessman from Birmingham who left a legacy of £50,000 specifically for the building of new lifeboats. Nineteen boats were built with this money, all bearing the same name but with a different number. *James Stevens No14* was one of the earliest lifeboats to be fitted with an engine and is now the world's oldest surviving motor lifeboat. She was moored alongside the pier which rendered the lifeboat house redundant – it is now a maritime museum.

DOGGERLAND

Doggerland appeals to the imagination in much the same way as the lost island of Atlantis. The difference is that Doggerland really is a lost country; it is still there under the sea, although its human inhabitants are long gone. Study a chart of the North Sea and you are looking at a map of Doggerland. The shoals and sandbanks marked on the chart were once the hills and ridges of dry land. My old Admiralty chart marks the depth of water over much of the North Sea as being generally between ten and twenty fathoms, but there is a large area between Flamborough Head on our east coast and northern Holland, marked on the chart as Outer Silver Pit, where the water is up to forty fathoms deep. This was once a vast lake in Doggerland, fed by rivers which are now gone but can apparently still be detected as channels in the seabed if you have the right equipment. The bed of the North Sea is well known to the fishermen who fish its waters for plaice, bass and sole, knowing where different fish like to make their home, and it is becoming familiar now to geologists

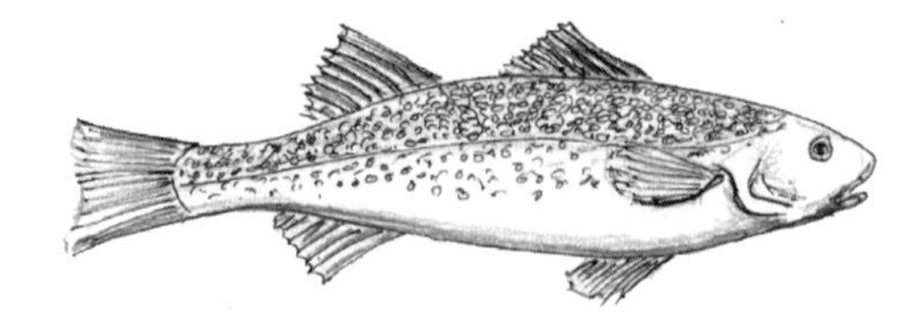

above Plaice; *right* Sea bass
opposite A sole disappears off the page

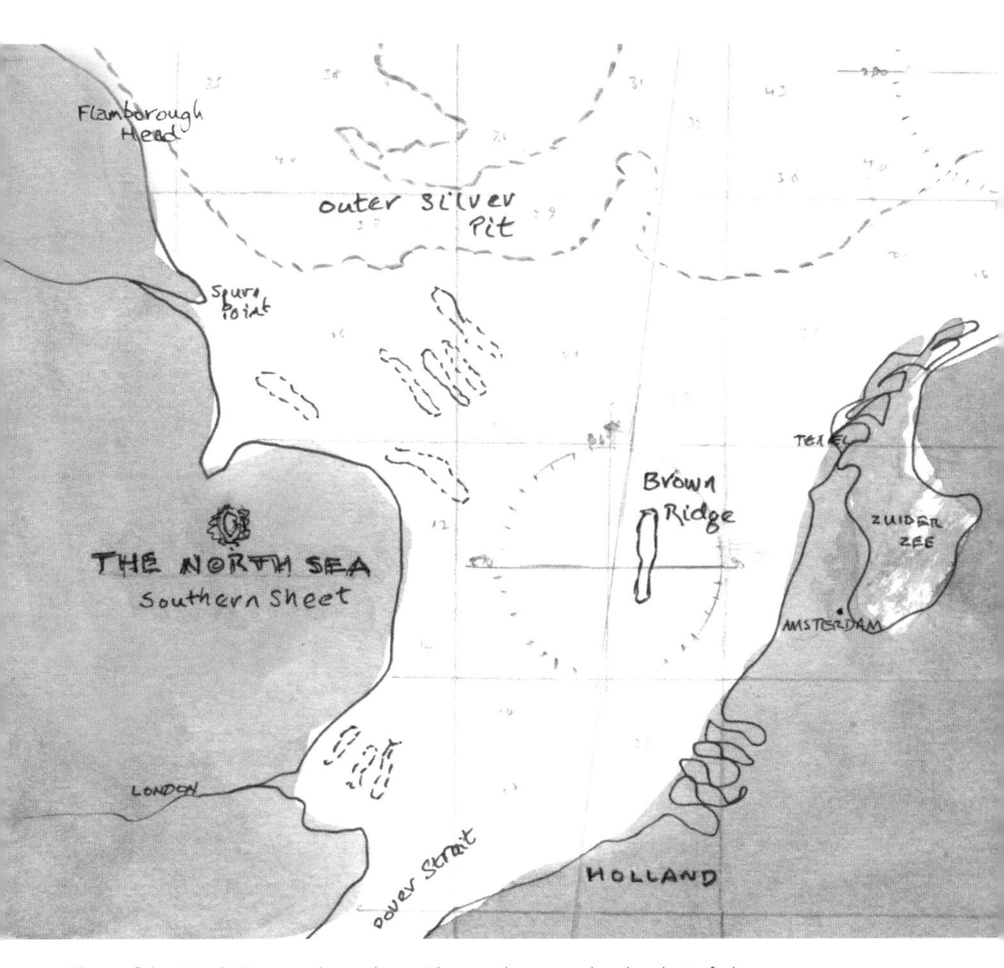

Chart of the North Sea, southern sheet. The numbers are the depths in fathoms

surveying for natural resources: their mapping provides an accumulating mass of information about the geography and the nature of this country now lost to us.

Beam trawling for bottom-feeding fish has a long and at times controversial history. The trawl net is dragged across the seabed, its mouth held open by a heavily weighted beam which scrapes along the bottom, destroying everything in its path. But over the years beam trawling did not just bring up plaice and sole: from time to time a strange item – a large tusk, a bone, a piece of antler – would appear in the net. These were of no interest to the fishermen, who mostly threw them back, but the presence of these unexplained artefacts was common knowledge among fishing folk. In 1985 a fisherman gave to Dick Mol, a Dutch palaeontologist, a human jawbone that was subsequently found to date from the Mesolithic age; now palaeontologists began to realise the possibility that the land under the North Sea may once have been inhabited by humans. Since then, many more artefacts have been dragged up and archaeologists are gradually piecing together evidence of a Mesolithic people who once lived and hunted in this forgotten world. It was named Doggerland by Professor Bryony Cole of Exeter University, who led the initial research into this area for many years.

Pinning down the detail of events that happened over the past twenty millennia is never going to be easy, and the information discovered by underwater archaeologists is emerging piecemeal, but a picture of the lost country under the North Sea is gradually coming into focus.

The sequence and the causes of those events is a combination of evidence and conjecture. Mapping a lost world speaks to the imagination as well as to the science, and it often takes a creative leap from the evidence to gain a greater understanding. You will find no finer description of what this hidden land could have been like than in *Time Song: Searching for Doggerland*, in which the author, Julia Blackburn, can turn an archaeological paper into captivating poetry. Her book is one long, beautiful riff on Doggerland.

Imagine a frozen world where an ice sheet several miles deep lies over the northern hemisphere. Nothing grows, all is still. This is how our world was at the beginning of the Quaternary period 2.5 million years ago. But the earth is moving gradually nearer the sun on one of its long cycles and very slowly the ice begins to release its frozen water. Sea levels start to rise and land appears at the edge of the glacier. This land is tundra. The subsoil remains frozen all year round – we call this permafrost – but during the short summer, grasses and other plants can sustain large grazing mammals such as mammoths, oxen and horses, all of which grow shaggy coats to protect them from the cold. No trees grow here – the growing season is too short for that – but as the climate continues to warm up, these hairy grazing mammals follow the retreating tundra north and mammals from the more temperate regions in the south

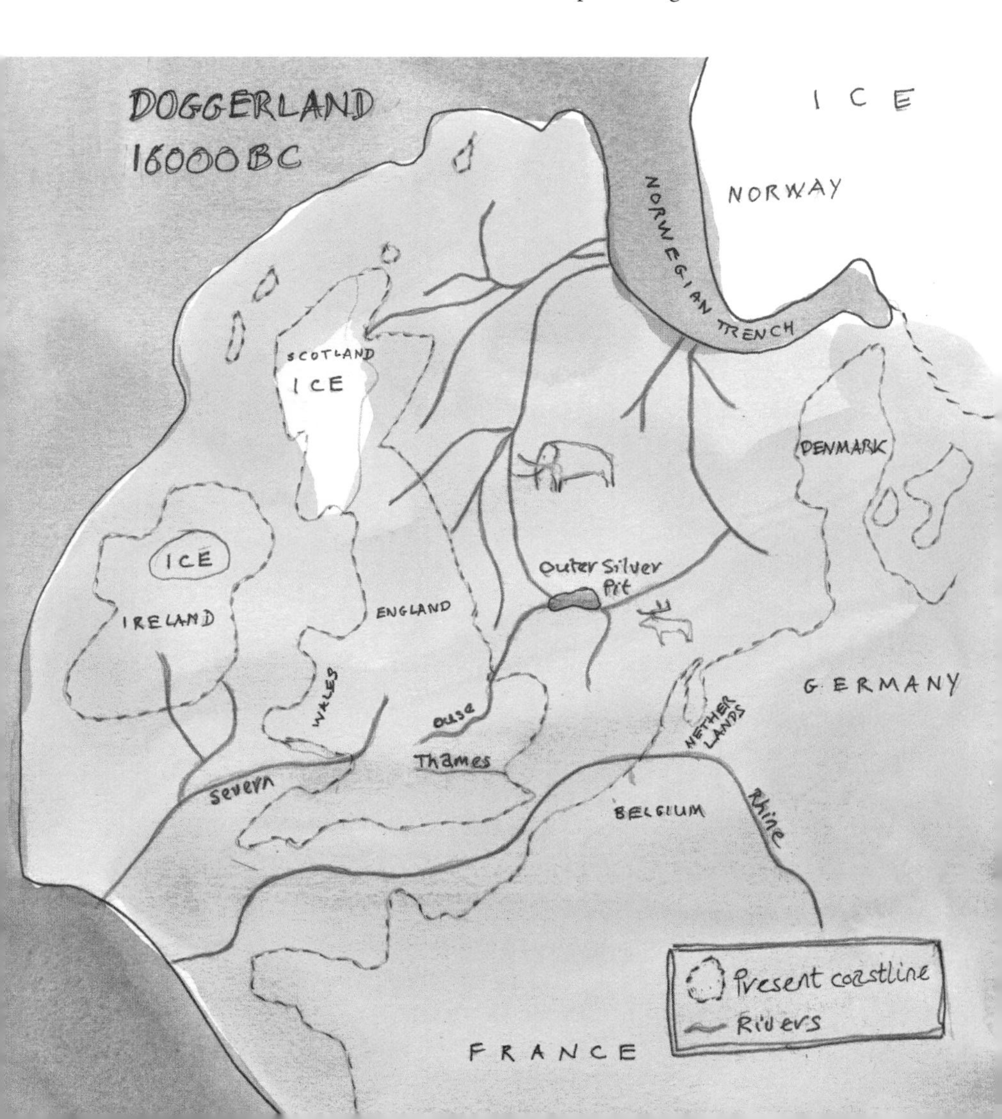

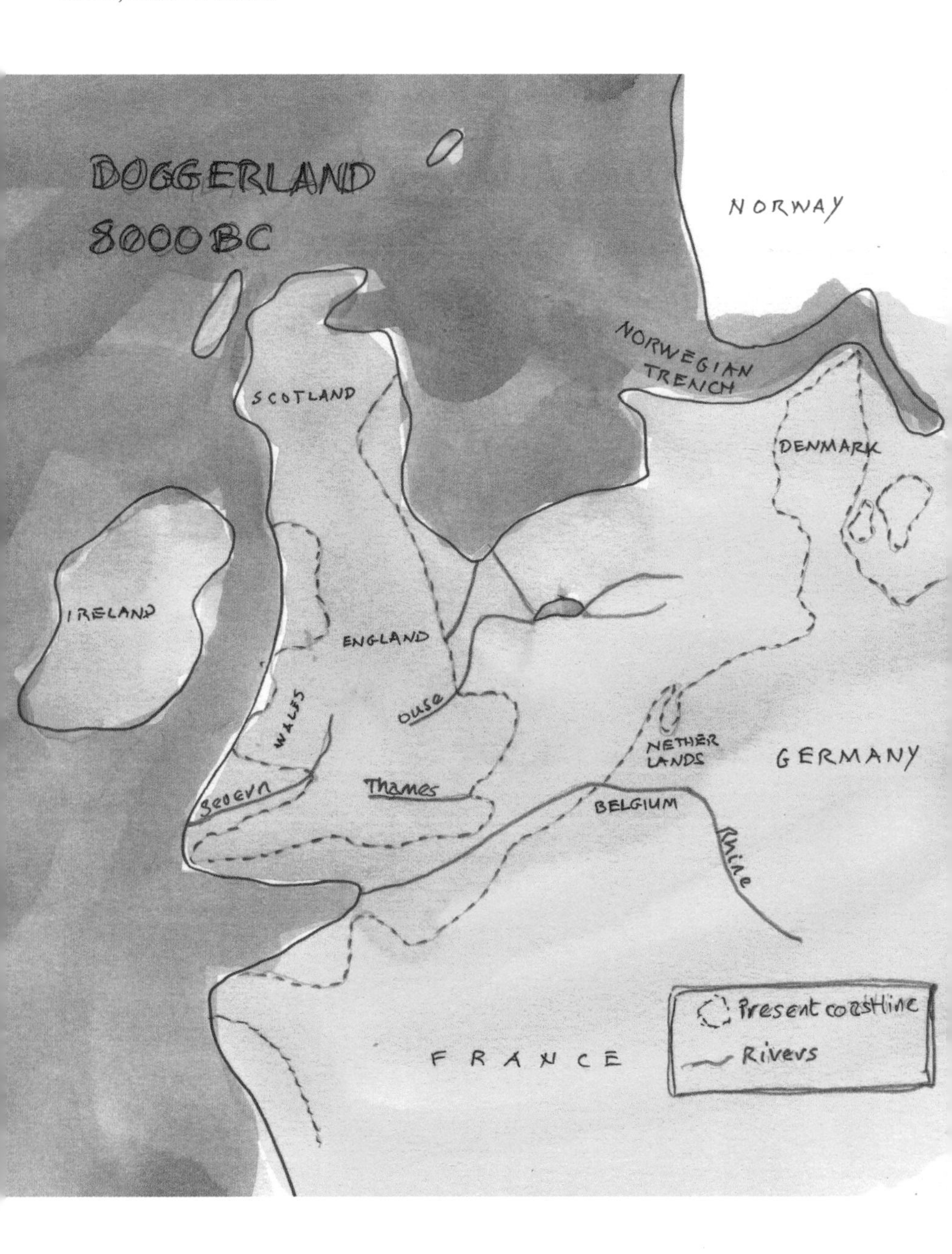
DOGGERLAND
8000 BC
NORWAY
NORWEGIAN
TRENCH
SCOTLAND
DENMARK
IRELAND
ENGLAND
WALES
Ouse
NETHER
LANDS
GERMANY
Severn
Thames
BELGIUM
Rhine
FRANCE
Present coastline
Rivers

migrate into what is now gradually becoming woodland. Willow, oak and elm have started growing. The reindeer have gone north now, following the ice, but red deer, elk and wild boar have moved in to replace them.

It is now 11,500 years ago, the passing of the Pleistocene into the Holocene epoch, and hominids are on the move. The North Sea has yet to form and Britain is still just the westernmost edge of Europe. Doggerland has now become a rich hunting ground for the semi-nomadic Mesolithic people who move across Europe following the animals they depend on for food and vital commodities such as skins for clothing and shelter, sinews for rope, and bone and antler for tools. It is a large plain with gentle hills, rivers and lakes, marshland and wooded valleys: ideal territory for any hunter-gathering people, and from the increasing amount of evidence – animal bones showing signs of having been butchered, tools made from flints and antlers, the occasional human bone – it is clear that Doggerland was once an inhabited country. Underwater archaeology is expensive and difficult to carry out, but there are other places in Northern Europe where signs of Mesolithic human settlements are still sometimes exposed during very low tides and, being more accessible, these sites are much easier to study. Goldcliff on the Severn Estuary is one of these. Long ago, when the river Severn was deep and narrow, oak trees grew widely in its environs and evidence shows that mesolithic people made encampments on the shore. But sea levels were rising and the river banks began to flood, first creating a scattering of small islands and then forming the wide estuary we are familiar with now.

Over the centuries the people who returned to these camps year after year would have found their landscape changing. The oak forests flooded and they learned the skills of trapping fish in the water and marshes. Sea levels in those times were rising at a rate of about three to six feet every hundred years or so. This would make for a great deal more loss of land on the flatter, eastern side of what is now Britain, where Doggerland would have been shrinking in size and changing to a much more marshy landscape. In Mesolithic times the nomadic way of life of the Palaeolithic age was gradually changing into the more settled farming life of the Neolithic age. Evidence has been found of gatherings of large numbers of people from time to time, when information and news could be exchanged and social interaction between families and tribes could take place. Their camps were not abandoned but were returned to at different times of year as the groups followed their food sources through the seasons.

Doggerland was shrinking inexorably and worse was yet to come.

A vast glacial lake in North America was melting and in around 6200 BC it released so much water into the Atlantic that the ocean rose by two feet. This icy cold water interfered with the warm currents in the North Atlantic, which in turn caused temperatures to plummet in Europe. But if the melting of the North American lake made life harsher for Mesolithic people here, another devastating blow was yet to come from the direction of Norway. One hundred years after this rise in sea level, a large piece of the Norwegian sea shelf slipped – one of the series of Storegga slides – causing a tsunami to sweep south towards the coast of northern Europe, flooding the great plain of Doggerland. The newly formed sea created a Britain-shaped peninsula, now only attached at its south-eastern corner to the rest of Europe.

This was the birth of the North Sea and the end of Doggerland.

A ROUGH GUIDE TO GEOLOGY

The earth was formed a long 4,500 billion years ago, but more recent geological time has been divided into three great *eras*, each subdivided into *periods*, some of which are further divided into *epochs*. The three eras are the Palaeozoic, the Mesozoic and the Cenozoic, and there has been a mass extinction during each one.

The **Palaeozoic era** (570 to 250 million years ago) is the oldest and is divided into the Cambrian, Ordovician, Silurian, Devonian, Carboniferous and Permian periods.

570 million years ago, single-celled organisms in the sea began to form themselves into more complex structures, and it was in the Devonian period (395 to 345 million years ago) that the first fish evolved.

If the Devonian was the age of the fish, the Carboniferous period (345 to 280 million years ago) was the age where life emerged on to land as some of the fish were adapting to live partially out of the water, and the first trees appeared.

The **Mesozoic era** (250 to 65 million years ago), the age of the reptiles, is divided into the Triassic, Jurassic and Cretaceous periods.

The Triassic period (250 to 200 million years ago) was the age of marine reptiles and of those most familiar of prehistoric creatures, the ammonites. The Jurassic period (200 to 140 million years ago) began the age of the dinosaurs and other land reptiles. Sea levels rose, tectonic plates shifted, and the great land mass of Pangaea began to break up.

The Cretaceous period (140 to 65 million years ago) saw the appearance of the first flowering plants and small mammals. But as the period drew to an end, a great asteroid collided with the Earth and the resulting dust cloud blotted out the sun for many years, causing the mass extinction which was the end of the dinosaurs.

The **Cenozoic era** (65 million years ago to the present), the age of the mammals, is divided into the Tertiary and Quaternary periods. There were no more dinosaurs, but some of the smallest mammals managed somehow to cling on to life in this new cold, inhospitable environment, and as the earth began to warm up again, long-buried seeds stirred into life. With the warmth came enough light for photosynthesis and, stretching their leaves towards the sun, the plants grew lush and strong and the great cycle of life began to turn once more. The surviving morganucodontids, tiny shrew-sized mammals that had lived precariously among the mighty dinosaurs, could now feed on plentiful leaves, fruits and seeds again. No longer prey to large carnivorous reptiles, they were free to evolve unhindered, and a great diversity of mammals came to populate all corners of the earth.

The Quaternary period (2.6 million to 11,500 years ago) is subdivided into the Pleistocene and the Holocene epochs, and it is in the Pleistocene, known also as the Ice Age, that early human beings first appear. We are getting closer to home. Some say we are now in a third stretch of time they call the Anthropocene, such is the impact that humans have had on the earth.

An ammonite

A CLOSER LOOK AT THE QUATERNARY PERIOD

2.6m years ago, the continents of our world were more or less where they are now and an ice sheet covered a large part of the northern hemisphere. This ice sheet retreated and advanced again as global temperatures rose and fell in cycles that depended on how close the Earth was to the sun. The Earth does not move around the sun in a perfect circle and when it is at its furthest from the sun it cools, warming up again as it gets closer. This cycle takes about 100,000 years. The earth also tilts on its axis in a cycle of 41,000 years and wobbles over a 23,000-year cycle. When all the cold-inducing factors come together we enter a glacial period, and when the warmth-inducing factors line up we enter an interglacial time like the one we are in now. In glacial periods much water becomes locked up as ice and consequently sea levels fall, opening up land bridges which allow the migration of animals and humans.

As ice melts and retreats, sea levels rise again and the revealed landscape, once hidden under glaciers many metres deep, shows the scars made in the rock by the sheer weight of the moving ice. During the Quaternary, the mammals which had adapted for survival in colder temperatures followed the ice northwards and many eventually became extinct, as their tundra habitat disappeared and humans became more adept at hunting them for food. The most recent ice age ended about 10,000 years ago and mammals from warmer southern latitudes began to move up into northern Europe.

A ROUGH GUIDE TO EARLY HUMANS

While geologists measure time in many millions of years and classify it into geological periods, archaeologists use a cultural classification for the development of humans.

When I first asked the question 'When did the mesolithic period begin and end?', I had no idea I was venturing into the vast field of the cultural development of man. When I asked the question 'How did *Homo sapiens* evolve?' I found myself immersed in yet another, equally fascinating study of the evolution of primates in Africa into various versions of early man, of which *Homo* was only the most recent. Growing up in the sixties I remember the excitement of reading about the finding of the first hominids in Africa, when Richard Leakey became famous for discovering fossils of *Australopithecus* in the Olduvai Gorge in East Africa. Many more hominid fossils have been unearthed there since and *Australopithecus* was just one branch of human-like primates. It was with the emergence of another genus, *Homo,* that we start to get closer to our own species, *Homo sapiens,* modern man.

OUR EARLY ANCESTORS

There is no firm consensus among archaeologists when it comes to classifying early humans, but it is agreed that it is during the Pleistocene, the time of the Ice Ages, when the ancestors of our species, *Homo sapiens,* first started to appear in the fossil record. Some palaeontologists classify *Homo* into just four or five species, while others split them further into eight (the scientists are cheerfully referred to as 'lumpers' and 'splitters'). These ancestors are *Homo habilis*, *H. rudolfensis*, *H. ergaster*, *H. erectus*, *H. antecessor*, *H. floresiensis* and *H. heidelbergensis*, the latter being the putative common ancestor of both *H. sapiens* and *H. neanderthalensis*. With the exception of *neanderthalensis*, all of them started off in Africa and moved from there into Eurasia, crossing on foot over land bridges now long gone. It was the European branch of *H. heidelbergensis* which later went on to develop into *H. neanderthalensis,* which is why Neanderthals are only found here in Europe.

Who were the Neanderthals?

Rather needing to be rescued from the popularly held image of the dim, ape-like cave man, the Neanderthals were skilled at making stone tools, they lived in social groups and they made art. The Neanderthals overlapped with our species for about 6,000 years, and there are many questions still to be answered about why they died out. Was it through combat or competition with modern humans for resources? It is not even certain whether the two species came across one another very much, let alone whether they interbred significantly. There is a theory that modern man was simply much better than his Neanderthal neighbour at forming the social networks which could give mutual support in times of hardship.

Homo sapiens first appears 200,000 years ago, spreading out from Africa to eventually occupy all the continents of the world, with the exception of Antarctica. The story of how they did this is still being gradually pieced together, but as sea levels rose and fell at different times in the past, land bridges would have opened up between continents that are now separated by seas, allowing tribes of our nomadic ancestors to move further and further afield in search of food to be gathered and animals to be hunted. As we have seen, it was in the Pleistocene period that modern man first appeared, gradually spreading around the world and eventually reaching Europe about 45,000 years ago. They were a nomadic hunter-gatherer people, following herds of large grazing animals, hunting and foraging for food, and making the flint tools that gave the name of Stone Age to their culture.

The Stone Age

The earliest period of the stone age, the **Palaeolithic**, is subdivided into three more stages, largely defined by the tools they used. In the earliest, the **Lower Palaeolithic**, the main tool was the hand-axe. A flint the size of a man's hand was skilfully chipped into a tear shape, tapering on two sides to a sharp edge; the resulting axe head fitted beautifully into the hand and would have had multiple uses. This bi-faced type of tool is known as Acheulian, after the place in France where such implements were first described, and dates from 1.7 million years ago.

In the **Middle Palaeolithic,** 250,000 years ago, the tools were of much greater variety and no longer bi-faced. They were often made from prepared 'tool blanks'. Polished areas on the surface are signs that they were hafted on to a shaft of bone, wood or antler for use as spears. Analysis of human bones from this time indicates that more meat was being eaten: man was changing from a scavenger into a hunter. It is within this time span that hearths first appear; another cultural milestone was passed as man learned to control fire.

In the **Upper Palaeolithic,** 50,000 years ago, tools became more diverse. Spear throwers, much like the ball throwers used by dog owners now, could turn a spear into a missile, killing from a distance, which was considerably safer than getting up close with a large animal. The bow and arrow also made its appearance in the Upper Palaeolithic, cave art flourished, shelters were now being built and the dead were interred in graves.

The **Mesolithic** and **Neolithic** periods saw much faster changes. The Palaeolithic had lasted unchanging for thousands of years, but a seismic shift happened when the idea of staying in one place and growing food, instead of always moving on to search for it, began to take hold. Farming first began about 12,000 years ago in the area known as 'the fertile crescent' in the Middle East, a crescent-shaped area spanning Egypt to the Persian Gulf. This new way of life moved slowly westwards from there but did not really take hold in north-west Europe until 6,000 years later. The intermediate stage between the old Palaeolithic (hunting and gathering) culture and the new Neolithic (farming) culture is known as the Mesolithic period. This means that the date at which these cultures begin and end is dependent upon which part of the world one is talking about. This same qualification is needed when looking at the timing of the Bronze Age and the Iron Age. Acquisition of the knowledge of how to smelt copper and tin to make the alloy of bronze did not reach Britain from mainland Europe until around 2500 BC, and iron-forging expertise did not arrive until as late as 500 BC.

Farming

There is much still to be discovered about how farming spread around the world. Was it the physical movement of people bringing their knowledge of horticulture with them, or was it more a cultural diffusion of the idea? Maybe it was a mixture of both, but however it came about, it is hard to overestimate the cultural effect on a previously nomadic people who were now staying in one place and growing their food, thus enabling an unprecedented growth in population.

Small family groups who were always on the move, living on a varied diet and treading lightly on the land, were changing into people living in small settlements with many more mouths to feed. They were soon dependent on successful harvests, and in times of drought the concept of famine appeared. The once varied nomadic diet was reduced now to those crops which could be grown easily, and we became dependent on a monoculture of wheat, or one of rice in other parts of the world. Farming was much harder work, too: land had to be cleared, stones picked from the fields, crops harvested and stored for the winter, and, most importantly, land now 'belonged' to people. The labour of farming also meant less time for social activities and, as the size of a settlement grew, so all the complexities of life increased: of sharing land and possessions, of defending territory, of the spread of disease, and of working out rules by which we can all live together peaceably.

Cornwall is one of the few places in the world where tin is found, and tin mining became a major part of the Bronze Age economy

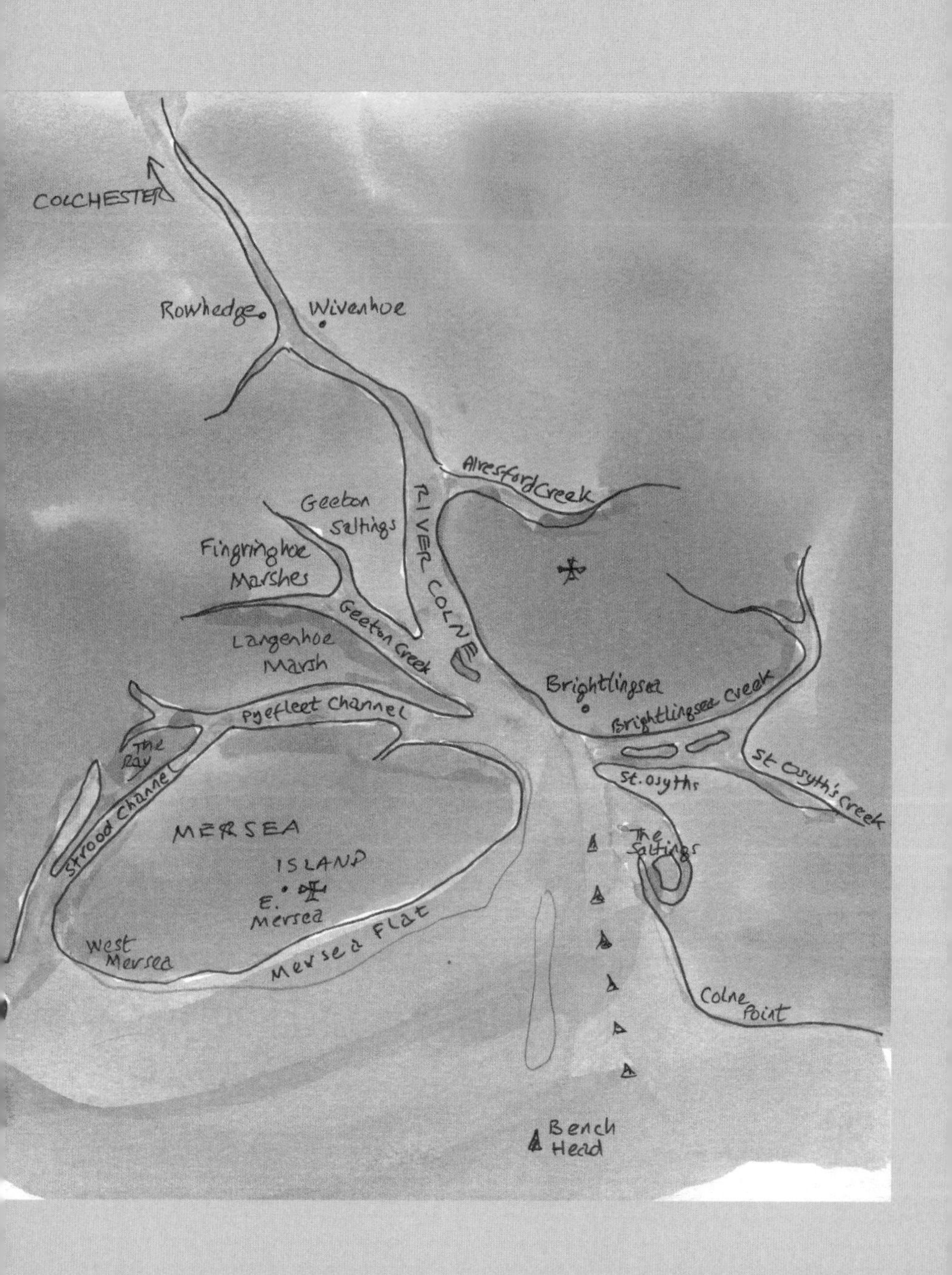

COLCHESTER
Rowhedge
Wivenhoe
Alresford Creek
RIVER COLNE
Geedon Saltings
Fingringhoe Marshes
Geedon Creek
Langenhoe Marsh
Brightlingsea
Brightlingsea Creek
Pyefleet Channel
The Ray
Strood Channel
St Osyth's Creek
St. Osyths
The Saltings
MERSEA ISLAND
E. Mersea
West Mersea
Mersea Flat
Colne Point
Bench Head

THE RIVER COLNE

THE RIVER COLNE

BRIGHTLINGSEA

For centuries Brightlingsea looked towards the sea for a living. Surrounded on three sides by streams and creeks making it practically an island, its only connection with the mainland is still the narrow spit of land that carries the B1029. This is rather neatly summed up by Sean O'Dell in his book *Skillingers of Brightlingsea*, when he writes 'if the sea was its front door, the land is its tradesman's entrance'. The deep water here allowed ships access to the shore at any stage of the tide and there is evidence of a dry dock, at the site of the old Aldous Boatyard, going back as far as the sixteenth century.

Like many of the towns around the Blackwater estuary, Brightlingsea's economy was based on oyster fishing. The inshore oyster smacks were up to forty-five feet long, thirteen foot in the beam and were built with an elegant cutaway stern, known as a *counter stern*, which effectively extended the deck space. The deck itself was free of any superstructure and, apart from space set aside in the forepeak for three berths and a stove, the rest of the room below was for storing the oysters which had to be brought back to port quickly to be sold alive. These smacks were built to provide maximum room on the deck for handling the dredge, as well as plenty of storage below for holding the catch. Speed was equally important and these highly effective, fast boats were generally back in port at the end of each day.

As the eighteenth century drew to a close, the demand for oysters had become so great that the local oyster beds were no longer productive enough to keep up with the market. The fishermen had to venture further afield and the best oyster grounds were to be found on the Terschelling Sands, just off the Dutch coast. It was a hazardous place to fish from, often on the lee side of the North Sea winds, and with no harbour nearby to take shelter from bad weather, many a fisherman lost his life here. The Brightlingsea boatyards built bigger, more robust smacks for the Terschelling fishery and these came to be known as *skillingers*, a corruption of Terschelling. They had better accommodation for the crew and a deep wet-well amidships to house a tank which could keep the oysters alive until they got home. Equipped with these improvements, the skillingers were able to venture much further afield and often went round the coast as far as Cornwall and over to France.

Skillingers were generally seventy feet long and carried two foresails on a long bowsprit, making them cutter-rigged.

The Boadicea*, a skillinger built in Maldon in 1815, is still sailing and was lying across the harbour at Brightlingsea when I was there*

The Aldous Boatyard closed in 1988 and now, as the Aldous Heritage Smack Dock, it is the home to the Colne Smack Preservation Society.

All Saints Church stands on raised ground a mile or so inland from the town, set in a large churchyard planted with trees. Giving views across fields to the west, it breathes an atmosphere of peacefulness and serenity. From the outside, it is the tower reaching high towards the sky that leaves the most

left Sketch of ceramic tile

opposite Map of the Cinque Ports and some of their limbs

vivid impression, seconded only by the beautiful flintwork of its walls. In 1872 Arthur Pertwee, a young clergyman, was installed here as vicar – he was to remain for forty years. A man of great compassion, he would sometimes go to sea with the fishermen in his parish to gain some understanding of the hardship and dangers they had to face. On stormy nights, well into his older years, he would bicycle up to the church and spend the night on top of the tower with a lantern to help guide the returning boats home. There was a terrible storm one day in March 1883, during which two hundred lives were lost up and down the North Sea coast, including thirty-six men from Brightlingsea. This tragedy gave him the idea of commemorating all the Brightlingsea men who had drowned at sea, going back to when he first arrived among them in 1872. He commissioned ceramic tiles to be made, recording the name, date and boat of each man who lost his life at sea: there are now 212 of these tiles in a frieze around the nave.

Life was changing for many of the towns along this stretch of coast as the nineteenth century turned to the twentieth. The oyster beds were failing and demand for oysters was waning as their association with typhoid fever was becoming apparent. The economy turned instead towards dredging for scallops, fishing for sprats, and the building and crewing of the new racing yachts.

Between the wars Brightlingsea was landing eighty per cent of the sprats caught along the east coast. The little fish were salted in brine and various flavourings added such as hops, cloves and bayleaves, or they were smoked in one of the many smokehouses that grew up in Brightlingsea at the time. After soaking in brine for six or seven hours, the fish were threaded on to

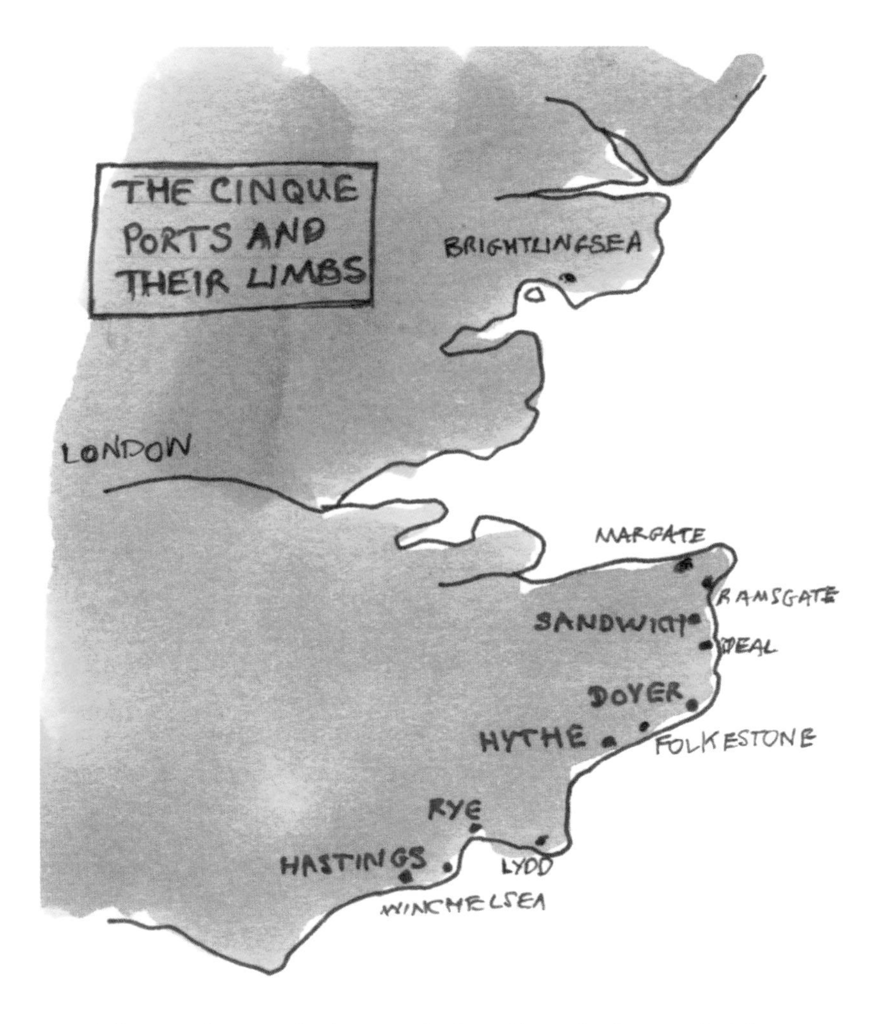

metal skewers then smoked over oak chips from the boatyards. They were exported in large quantities to Scandinavia, Germany, Poland and Russia, but fishing on this scale inevitably exhausted the stocks, which have never really recovered.

The Confederation of Cinque Ports

Given their charter in 1155, the Cinque Ports were five ports on the south-east coast granted privileges by the king in return for supplying ships for his

left Brightlingsea still bears the coat of arms of Sandwich, but with the three ship hulls in silver instead of gold

use in the days before we had a Royal Navy. Between them the ports were required to maintain fifty-seven ships, each ready with a crew of twenty-one men, for fifteen days service a year. The charter gave each port the rights to collect local taxes and to hold their own courts of justice, priority fishing rights over the herring and, most controversially of all, rights over the Herring Fair at Great Yarmouth.

The main herring breeding grounds moved to the banks off Great Yarmouth in the fourteenth century, and Yarmouth's herring fishery became renowned throughout the whole of Europe. A fair in medieval times was a big annual event and the Herring Fair at Great Yarmouth went on for several days, bringing merchants from all over Europe to trade in the salted and smoked herrings which were a staple food in those days. The resentment felt by the Yarmouth men towards the Cinque Port bailiffs would often spill over into fights, which sometimes led to loss of life.

The five original head ports of the Confederation were Hastings, New Romney, Hythe, Dover and Sandwich. Subsidary ports known as 'limbs' were later added, and two Ancient Towns, Rye and Winchelsea, were also required to have ships ready for defence. As their harbours silted up over the years, towns such as New Romney, Winchelsea and Tenterden lost their status and were replaced as they became stranded inland. Brightlingsea became a limb of Sandwich and is the only town in the Confederation of Cinque Ports north of the Thames Estuary, all the others being on the Kent and south coasts.

St Osyth

The village of St Osyth lies on the other side of Brightlingsea Creek. As I walked down to the water one evening my eye was caught by the extraordinary sight of a towering, flint-faced, fifteenth-century gatehouse which would not have looked out of place in Hampton Court. It was arresting, not only for its sheer size and magnificence, but for the fact that it did not appear to be leading anywhere. Standing incongruous and alone it gave no clue as to what it was inviting entrance to. This is all that is left now of St Osyth's Priory. Founded in 1121 for an order of Augustinian canons, it was once the largest religious house in Essex. After the dissolution of the monasteries it was granted to Thomas Cromwell for a while and since then has changed hands many times. There is little of the original monastic building left within the grounds now and the residential buildings there are mostly of Georgian origin. But the story of St Osyth goes back much further than that. Osyth was betrothed to Sighere, the king of the East Saxons, and legend says that at their wedding feast her husband caught sight of a white stag and, calling his men, he abandoned the feast to go hunting. This put the innocent young Osyth off the whole idea of marriage, and after producing a son for him she founded a nunnery at the nearby village of Chich, now known as St Osyth. The site of this much earlier priory is thought to lie in Nun's Wood, where a possible moated site and a series of fishponds have been found.

One night in 653 it was attacked by a band of raiding Danes. Osyth faced down the chief and rejected his demands, whereupon he ordered his men to behead her. She is said to have then calmly picked up her head and walked with it to the nearby chapel before finally collapsing, and now she haunts Nun's Wood, where she can sometimes be seen walking with her head tucked under her arm.

St Denis, patron saint of Paris, was also said to have picked up and walked with his head after his execution and he can be found carved beside the doorway on Notre Dame Cathedral, still holding his head under one arm. In fact a sufficient number of saints have done this for the word cephalophore to be coined to describe them. The head-carrying saints have always presented a problem for artists required to paint or carve them, as they don't know where to put the halo.

ROWHEDGE

The river Colne flows through Colchester, the city the Romans made their first capital in Britain before they moved it to London. The quayside at Colchester Hythe that once served the shipping trade for the Romans, is now an industrial area; this stretch of the river is now a peaceful one, running from Colchester towards the Blackwater Estuary, passing through the villages of Wivenhoe and Rowhedge, which lie on opposite banks.

As I arrived in Rowhedge to walk along the riverside footpath, a pair of redshanks were darting upriver and a solitary egret was pecking around in the mud across the water. The silence was broken only by the cries of the black-headed gulls, already beginning to lose the black caps they had sported all summer. The neatly mown village green and well-kept weather-boarded houses give the place an air of prosperity now, and residential homes have been built along the riverbank where the boatyards once were. The endless quiet rhythm of the tidal water ebbing and flowing through this rather sleepy village gave no indication of a former time when the small cottages were home to the fishermen and shipwrights working from the many boatyards which stretched along this side of the river. Two hundred years ago, or more, Rowhedge was a busy, active and far more noisy place than this. The yards were building smacks for oyster-dredging, schooners for trading and latterly sailing yachts for the wealthy men who were discovering the delights of cruising and racing. In 1909, when the Rowhedge Ironworks Company arrived, they started to build steel ships, too, and minesweepers for the Royal Navy during the second world war.

Minesweepers' hulls were built of composite wood and aluminium so they were not magnetic

Rowhedge Quay

Margaret Leather's father owned and sailed the fishing smack *Beatrice*, and he captained one of the cruising yachts of the time. The name Leather will be familiar to anyone who is interested in the history of sail as her son, John, was to become a naval architect, designing a number of east-coast boats, and a well-known writer on maritime subjects. Margaret grew up in Rowhedge in the early 1900s and all her brothers and uncles were seafaring men, as were most of the men living there at the time. She records life in Rowhedge during the early part of the twentieth century in *Saltwater Village*, a book in which she relates some wonderful stories of smuggling, salvaging and the days of yacht racing, when Rowhedge was famous for its yacht builders and the sailors who were employed to sail them.

One of her many stories concerns John Spitty, who was both a fisherman and licensee of the Royal Oak, a pub which still stands by the river today. He was a bit of a rogue, owning several smacks as well as running a sideline in smuggling. He used a bedroom at the inn on one occasion to hide a consignment of Dutch cigars he had brought in, stacking the boxes up to resemble a dressing table then draping the lot with a piece of chintz to complete the deceit. When the Revenue men, who long suspected him of smuggling, came to search the inn they failed to find the cigars, but it was the final straw for his long-suffering wife, who thereafter refused to allow him to stash any of his illicit goods at the inn. He would get his coal on the cheap by sailing close to one of the collier brigs anchored in the river and shout a code phrase such as 'Can you dress a hat?', whereupon fish would be exchanged for an illicit load of coal. He had a reputation for fearlessness and once, when caught in a storm at sea, he set the small foresail in place of the mainsail and sent his crew below. He later claimed he had been washed overboard by one wave and washed back on board again by the next. When the men eventually emerged from below decks they found they had drifted across the North Sea to Dutch Heligoland.

The houses in Rowhedge all had high linen lines. The long poles were made from old topmasts or other spars and the washing was hauled up using old ship's blocks. On Sundays it was customary to fly a yacht ensign, burgee or Union Jack from the top.

Many of the yachts were crewed and captained by men from the Colne and each man was issued with a set of clothes for the season. This consisted of:

one navy blue reefer jacket
two pairs of navy blue trousers
two jerseys with the yacht's name embroidered over the chest
one cheesecutter cap
one sou'wester
one sunhat
one oilskin coat
one pair of canvas deck shoes
one pair of leather shoes

The four Paget Memorial Cottages in Rowhedge were built by Alfred Henry Paget, the Marquis of Anglesey, for the families of the men who crewed his yachts. Today the cottages are occupied by those families' descendants, who continue to live there rent-free with the stipulation that they pay their own council tax and must always keep a framed photograph of Alfred Paget on the wall.

Rowhedge was also known as East Doneyland

WIVENHOE

Across the river from Rowhedge lies the small town of Wivenhoe. It is possible to get some idea of the size of coastal towns in the past by looking at the number of ships they registered. Before Britain had the Royal Navy, local boats could be commandeered for use by the King for whichever war he was waging at the time, so it was in the interest of the town to declare fewer vessels than the true number for fear of losing them to become warships. However, in 1582 Wivenhoe officially declared twelve working boats, giving an approximate idea of its size, and by the end of that century the town also had two packet boats making regular trips from Wivenhoe to London, carrying cloth woven in East Anglia.

Roger Townsend (of the Townsends of Rainham, or Raynham, in Norfolk) held the Manor of Wivenhoe at the time of the Spanish Armada, and commanded the soldiers aboard one of the bigger ships, the Elizabeth Jonas

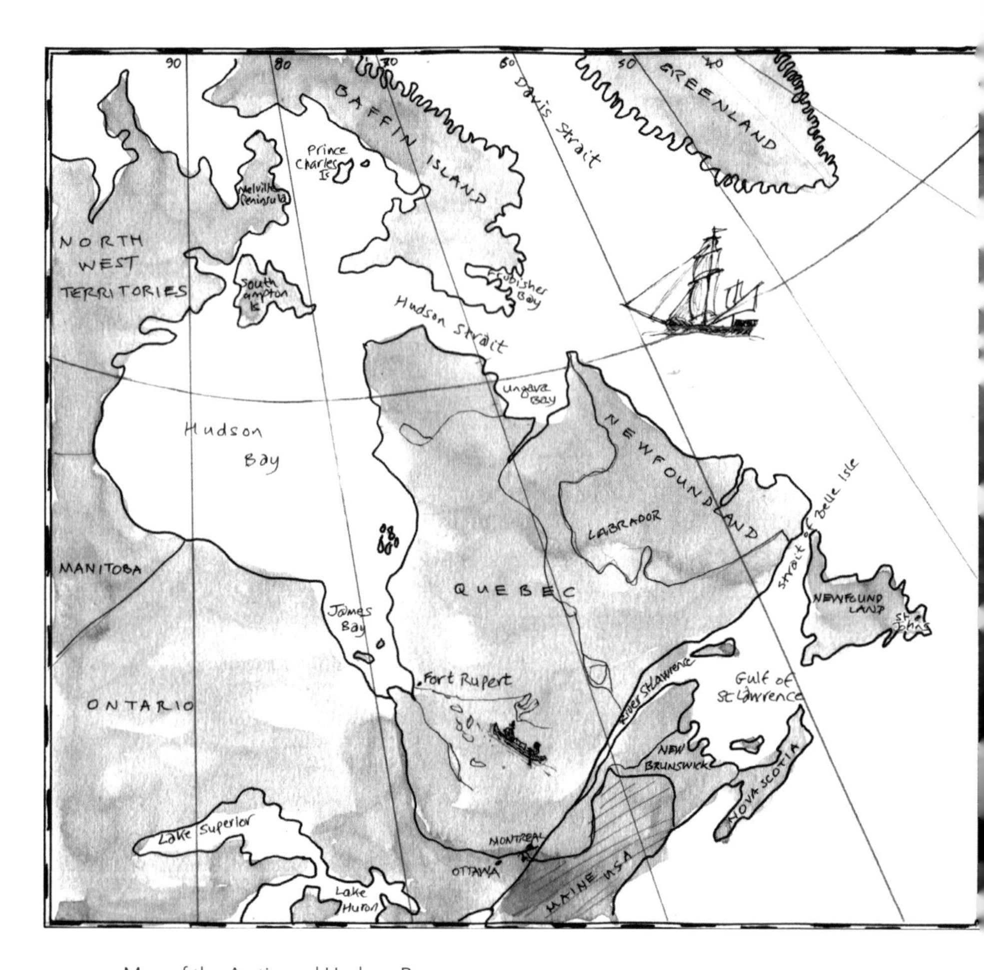

Map of the Arctic and Hudson Bay

THE VOYAGE OF THE *NONSUCH* AND THE HUDSON BAY COMPANY

One of Wivenhoe's well-known ships was the ***Nonsuch***, built there as a merchant ship in 1650. She was a ketch and so carried two masts, each bearing the square sails typical of the day, and she was to become famous many years later when she was bought by two adventurers who sailed her to Canada in 1668 in an attempt to open up the trade in beaver fur. But the story begins further back than that, when two men from New France (Quebec), in Canada, made the long journey by canoe through the Great Lakes to the fur-trading posts in the far north. Médard Sieur des Groseilliers was an experienced explorer and had led several expeditions crucial for French territorial claims in North America. He was accompanied by his brother-in-law, Pierre-Esprit Radisson, a man described by his biographer, Grace Lee Nute, as 'one of those fortunate people endowed with an unquenchable zest for life and a capacity for adaptation not too greatly hampered by religious, moral, or patriotic scruples'.

Beaver fur was highly prized for its warmth, and beavers were trapped and shot in large numbers. It is thought that the two men probably got as far as St James Bay, which lies at the southern end of Hudson's Bay. Their route through the rivers and forests of the far north, freezing in the winter and plagued with blackflies in the brief summer, would have been gruelling.

Having made the arduous journey to get there, they could see the potential of instead using ships, which could sail in and out of Hudson Bay in the warmer months when the bay was ice-free, making the journey by sea instead.

But on their return not only did they fail to get the support of the Governor of New France but they were promptly fined for trading without a licence. Undaunted, they sought sponsorship further afield, meeting some colonial British merchants in Boston. A pilot voyage failed due to problems with the pack ice and, reluctant to risk further financial loss but still recognising the scheme's potential, the merchants advised the two men to travel to England to seek help from the court. An introduction there to Prince Rupert soon led to sponsorship from Rupert's cousin, King Charles II, who was more than ready to seize a chance to get one over the French colony.

A small consortium of merchants then acquired the *Nonsuch* for the grand sum of £290. She set sail from Gravesend on 3 June 1668, captained by one Zachariah Gillam. Groseilliers sailed on the

Nonsuch, and Radisson was on the accompanying ship the *Eaglet*, which had to return after sustaining damage during a storm off the coast of Ireland. So the *Nonsuch* sailed on alone, past the Orkneys then turning westwards past Iceland and the southern tip of Greenland before sighting the Labrador coast on 1 August. Sailing through the Hudson Strait they finally entered St James Bay on 29 September, anchoring at the mouth of a river. They named the site Fort Rupert. It was already beginning to get cold and they built wooden cabins on the shore, settling in for a long winter waiting for the Indian traders. They bought as many beaver skins as they could but the ice would not allow the ship to leave for home until the following August. They reached Britain in October 1669, laden with valuable skins, having thus established a viable trade route to the far north. Prince Rupert and his fellow investors then approached the King for a charter permitting them to trade into the territory the *Nonsuch* had opened up. This was granted in May 1670 and the Hudson Bay Company was born.

Wivenhoe was settling down into an economy based on the universal maritime occupations of fishing, trading and the building of boats. Further, the wool trade, on which so much of Norfolk, Suffolk and Essex depended, began to decline as the effects of the Industrial Revolution began to bite. As local spinners and weavers were superseded by factory mills in the north of England, fishing for sprats and oysters became even more important.

By the beginning of the nineteenth century merchants were investing in ships for trade, now employing a captain and crew rather than sailing the vessels themselves. Twenty-eight of these merchant vessels were operating from Wivenhoe's wharves in 1805. The local shipyards had plenty of work building ships needed for the Napoleonic Wars in addition to the commercial boats, but an unexpected boost to the local economy was on the horizon. Its origins lay in the evolution of the east-coast fishing smacks.

It had always been an advantage to have a fast boat for fishing, as before the days of refrigeration the first boat back to shore would get the best price for its fish. In these tricky waters, however, it was just as important for a smack to have the speed and manoeuvrability to sail quickly off a dangerous lee shore, and of course a good turn of speed enabled them to outrun the Revenue cutters when indulging in a bit of smuggling. With such fast and handy boats it was only natural then for the fishermen to compete with each other and local regattas became popular in the summer months. This reputation for building fast boats brought the Colne boatbuilders to the attention of some of the wealthy men who were taking up the new sport of yacht racing in the early nineteenth century. One of key figures was Lord Henry Paget, Marquis of Anglesey. Paget had been second-in-command to Wellington at Waterloo, losing a leg along the way, and he was not prepared to settle for a dull life after that. He wanted a fast yacht and he wanted Philip Sainty to build it.

The colourful life of Philip Sainty

Philip Sainty, who sounds rather similar in character to John Spitty, the fisherman and licensee of the Royal Oak at Rowhedge, who we met earlier, had a reputation for building particularly fast boats, so this was the man Lord Paget decided should build him a racing yacht. But there was a problem. Sainty and his son, John, were languishing in Chelmsford jail, having been finally caught smuggling. Paget was not put off by such an inconvenience: he pulled a few strings and managed to get an order for Sainty's release. But the wily boatbuilder somehow managed to get the paperwork made out in the name of his son John instead. Falling neatly into the trap, the Marquis realised the error and had a second order made out in Sainty's name and so both father and son were freed. Sainty then went a step further and managed to engineer the release of his brother, who was in Maidstone jail on the same charges, by insisting that he could not possibly build his yacht without his brother's help.

Released from jail and together again, the Saintys built the *Emerald* for Paget, launching her in 1819, just six months after their release from prison. The sixty-one-foot cutter was built at Stuttles yard in Colchester and was followed a year later by the ninety-two-foot *Pearl.* Sainty went on to build several more yachts, signalling the start of a hundred years of yacht building in yards all along the river Colne. The boatbuilders of Wivenhoe, Rowhedge, Brightlingsea and Tollesbury not only built the yachts, but the local fishermen, skilled at handling fast boats and heavy sails, were employed during the summer months as crew and captains.

John Constable from East Bergholt joined the Royal Academy School as an apprentice in 1799

The *Pearl* was clearly a much loved vessel as the Marquis kept her for thirty-one years. He even persuaded the Royal Navy to commission Sainty to build a warship for them; she was taken round to the Royal Naval Dockyard at Woolwich for her final fitting-out: the three-masted vessel was also named *Pearl.*

When Philip Sainty's colourful life came to an end at the age of ninety, he left behind approximately eighteen children from three different wives and had been declared bankrupt twice.

To give some idea of the increasing size of the town, by the 1850s there were fifty-five smacks working from the quays, as well as ten billyboys, a local type of sailing barge, and at least a dozen merchant ships trading mainly in coal, but some were going as far as the West Indies and Canada. Wivenhoe was doing well.

Thomas Harvey bought Sainty's yard and, with his son John, built the *Volante* in 1849. The *Volante* was famous for racing the schooner *America* round the Isle of Wight in 1851 for the £100 cup donated by the Royal Yacht

Squadron – the origin of the America's Cup challenge (see the final chapter: The Rivers Crouch and Roach).

Thomas and his son went on to build more than fifty yachts, including the writer Edward Fitzgerald's yacht, the *Scandal,* which he sailed at Woodbridge, so named because nothing travels faster than scandal. Thomas retired to Brightlingsea in 1864 and made the yard over to John.

Edward Fitzgerald is best known today for his translation of The Rubaiyat of Omar Khayyam. *In Persian poetry, a rubaiyat is a poem of four-line stanzas.*

John Harvey used mathematical principles to design his yachts and was a founder member of the Institute of Naval Architects, going on to work with Lloyds of London to develop a method of classifying yachts based on their measurements. But although he had an excellent reputation and a busy workload, his brother Thomas, a partner in the business, proved to be a financial liability and the firm went bankrupt. All was not lost, however, and the John Harvey Yacht and Shipbuilding Company was formed in 1873. With John appointed as manager they were to enjoy ten prosperous years.

John hoped that his son, another John, would follow him into the trade, but he was cut from a different cloth, preferring instead to read, write and dream about joining the theatre. Fortunately for the boy his father had come to know WS Gilbert, who, after the success of *HMS Pinafore* in 1880, had commissioned a yacht from him. Harvey contacted the famous dramatist to see if he could help. Not only did Gilbert arrange for young John to train as an actor, but he later helped get him an audition. John Martin-Harvey went on to became an actor-manager – if you look up on the wall of the Rose and Crown pub in Wivenhoe, you will see a blue plaque commemorating him. John Harvey senior, meanwhile, had left the yard, emigrating to America to further his career, where he already had a reputation as a notable designer and builder.

By this time steel was beginning to replace wood for boatbuilding, and Forrest and Son took over the yard that had been run by Joseph Wilkins, a former apprentice of John Harvey. Joseph had built four Nile boats for General Gordon of Khartoum, but under the ownership of Forrest's the yard was now about to start building boats made of steel.

The steel boats built by Forrest's

Tern was a 140-foot passenger steamer destined for Lake Windermere. The boat was bolted together and then dismantled, each part carefully numbered, before it was packed up and taken to the Lake District by train for reassembling under the direction of one of the men from the yard. Several more were to follow her to Windermere: the *Esperance, Raven, Cygnet, Teal* and *Britannia.* Forrest and Son produced many more boats in this kit form, including one for the explorer Henry Morton Stanley, of Dr Livingstone fame. The riverboat they built for Stanley was 28 feet long and had no engine. She was powered instead by four pairs of oars and a lugsail, and was portaged in sections whenever they had to carry her overland between rivers.

Among the many other steel boats they built were three 140-foot vessels for Lord Kitchener, also for use in Africa. These were driven by a stern mounted paddle wheel and equipped with searchlights and guns. Two canoe sledges, for use in water as well as on the ice, were made for Arctic exploration, and a diving-bell barge was built for the Royal Navy in Gibraltar.

The *Tern*

THE POCKET SUBMARINE

Forrest's most unusual commission came when they were involved in the building of a miniature submarine in 1905. An article in the *Engineering Gazette* of November 1913 states that the electric motors and associated gear were made by Marryat and Place in London, and that she was designed by 'an eminent naval architect'. Quite who their customer was remains a mystery, but it is probably no coincidence that Japan was at war with Russia at the time.

Later dubbed 'the pocket submarine' by the *Daily Mail*, the *Volta* was built in secrecy, behind a screen in the corner of one of the sheds at Forrest's yard, and the man in charge of her construction was an American known as 'the professor'. At only thirty-four feet long and six feet nine inches in diameter, she could be carried on deck by a warship and lowered on davits for the purpose of delivering torpedoes underwater.

The *Volta* had a number of ingenious mechanisms. In order to submerge, water was pumped into ballast tanks and pumped out when she needed to surface. To keep her horizontal, a pendulum was linked through a switch to a travelling weight moving on runners down her length, immediately over the keel. This meant that the slightest deviation from horizontal was automatically corrected by the motor which adjusted the position of the weight. This system also allowed her to dive up or down at any chosen angle.

She was fitted with nine electric motors which would have given her a top speed of eight knots, but on her trials, the electromagnetic field they generated rendered the compass useless. Forrest's overcame this problem by designing of one of the first gyrostatic compasses. The British government, aware of her construction, was keen to keep the project in its sights and, hoping to prevent the *Volta*'s export, detailed the Colne River Police to keep a lookout for any of her movements. But the pocket submarine mysteriously disappeared and no one seems to have any idea of what became of her.

The story of the *Exact*

The *Exact* was a barge built at Colchester Hythe in 1959, so named because she fitted exactly under the Hythe bridge on her way downriver. In the early stages of her construction someone noticed that she looked too wide to get through the arch of the bridge, but to save starting all over again it was decided to 'kipper' her. This colourful term was coined to describe cutting her in half along her *kelson* (keel) to split her in two so her floors could be shortened, reducing her width. It must have been to save time that they only shortened the floors on one side. The story continues that the builders, worried that she may still be too wide, went down to the bridge at night with their adzes to reduce the width of the piers, just in case.

The Nottage Maritime Institute

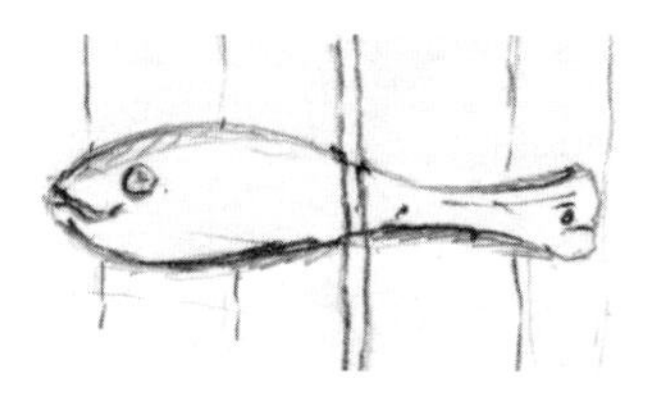

An old sail loft down on the waterfront is home to the unique Nottage Maritime Institute. Charles Nottage was born in 1852. His father made his money manufacturing the first cameras and went on to become Lord Mayor of London. After an education at Cambridge and working for four years as a barrister, Charles chose a more adventurous life. He walked through both central Russia and Japan, lived for a while in the South Seas, served in the army and was made a fellow of the Royal Geographic Society. The last four years of his life were blighted by a heart condition from which he died aged only 42, but his great love was sailing, and he owned and raced two yachts on the Colne, the *Foxhound* and the *Deerhound*. He grew to have a great respect for the fishermen of the Colne who crewed his yachts, and he left £13,000 in his will for the formation of a trust to educate the sons of these seafaring men. No longer needed for its original purpose, the Institute now teaches navigation to private boat owners, holds boatbuilding courses,

above right Door fastening of a smiley fish spotted in Wivenhoe

houses a collection of model ships, half-models and maritime paintings, and has an extensive library of books on maritime subjects.

SMUGGLING

If you were to stretch out the coastline of Essex, it would go on for many miles, for it has technically the longest coastline of any county in Britain. A map will make a clear demarcation between land and sea, but look at a nautical chart and it paints a different picture. Do you mean land at high water or low? Spring tides or neaps? Mersea is an island for only for an hour at every high tide. Wallasea, Canvey and Foulness are islands, but the separation of each one from the mainland is by no more than one of the many small waterways which snake their way to the sea, cutting the margins of the land into an intricate jigsaw puzzle.

It is the complexity and changing nature of this watery landscape that has always made it ideal territory for the tradition of smuggling. Where better for a fisherman to use his intimate knowledge of the channels and inlets where he could land a consignment of goods under cover of night to evade paying the steep duties imposed by the Crown?

The first customs duties

England in the Middle Ages, and particularly East Anglia, was famous throughout Europe for its fine wool. Bales of wool were exported mainly to the Low Countries, France and Italy, where it was dyed and woven into cloth. The cloth industry at that time was a large part of the economy across Europe and it was underpinned principally by the supply of high-quality wool from England. It was not just wool that was needed but also the alum used as a mordant, and dyestuffs which all had to be mined, shipped and dealt in the markets. The cloth industry thus provided employment for spinners, dyers, weavers and a host of other supporting industries, which in turn generated great wealth for all the merchants involved. The wool merchants of East

Anglia were responsible for building many of the large, beautiful churches in East Anglia which stand testimony still to this period in our history. So no surprise then that the first customs duties – initially levied at forty per cent by Edward I in 1275 – should be imposed on the export of wool. It was too tempting for both merchants and ship owners not to engage in 'free trade', otherwise known as smuggling.

Edward I had spent several years on a crusade before returning to England to be crowned King in 1274. He then set about conquering Wales.

At that time the collection of customs duties was farmed out to private individuals. The king issued an annual licence to a private individual who would pay an agreed sum of money each year to collect the tax. This ensured that the king received a set amount each year regardless of how much or how little the 'farmer' collected. It also gave the collector of the tax the incentive to pursue his task more rigorously.

The sixteenth century saw the increasing regulation of customs duties, with designated ports having legal or *sufferance* wharves where merchant ships were required to report to the Customs House before loading or unloading their goods. The system was shamelessly abused by everyone, however, and the local customs collectors were very often trading in their own right as merchants themselves. This all went on happily for a very long time until the Exchequer, singling out Ipswich and the ports of Essex as the worst offenders, overhauled the whole of the corrupt system. Doing away with the licensing of 'farmers' to collect taxes, the king in 1671 appointed six customs commissioners who were responsible for collecting the duties instead, and created a department of state responsible to the Treasury. The commissioners, based at their offices near the Tower of London, had control of all shipping and employed local customs officers at each port. These men were given privileges such as exemption from being pressed into the Royal Navy, which was a constant hazard for any seafaring man in those days. At least that was how it should have worked, but little actually changed very much, except that fights between customs officers and the 'owlers', as the wool dealers were called, became more frequent as the illegal trade continued to expand.

After the Glorious Revolution of 1688, when William and Mary came to replace James II on the throne, England was soon at war with France again. But wars were expensive and required more taxes to pay for them. A vicious spiral now ensued: as fast as customs duties were increased to raise more revenue, the more the smuggling increased to avoid paying it. The shipyards were by now building fast boats commissioned especially for smuggling: similar to the fishing smacks, these boats were fast, shallow-draughted and, with their fore and aft rig, highly manoeuvrable. They could sail into one of the hundreds of little creeks to load or unload their goods, and slip swiftly out to sea again without being detected. The Customs Board then began to invest in equally fast Revenue cutters, often built by the same boatbuilders, which they stationed in various ports around the coast. These were backed up with riding officers who patrolled the coast day and night on horseback and who in turn could call on the local mounted dragoons for help if necessary. For many years the Revenue fleet was second in size only to the Royal Navy.

Things could only get worse. In 1683 the government had thought up a new tax called the excise, which to begin with was a tax specifically for home-produced goods such as beer, malt, spirits, soap, candles and bricks. But when it was imposed on the import of French brandy in addition to the existing customs duty, smuggling became a problem for the excise too. In the ensuing years excise duty was slapped on to wine, spirits, tea, coffee, tobacco and sugar, and smuggling became even more ingrained. The excise collectors had their own fast sloops and were often better at catching the smugglers than their customs counterparts.

Smuggling was a deeply embedded part of life on the Essex coast for many years, the smugglers preferring to call themselves free traders. Graham

Smith, in his book *Smuggling in Essex*, records a report from 1736 stating that 'in some parts of the maritime counties the whole population is so generally engaged in smuggling that it is impossible to find a jury that will upon trial do justice to an officer of the Revenue in any case whatsoever'.

Until the nineteenth century contraband was usually landed on open beaches for carrying away by horsemen, but as the customs officers upped their game, it became more usual to sink the goods in wooden tubs for retrieval later. This was done by creeping: that is, by dragging grappling hooks known as creepers along the bottom to haul the the goods up. The tubs for this purpose were usually supplied already roped together in pairs so they could be slung over the shoulder for carrying away.

The marshes between the river Stour and Walton Naze were a paradise for smugglers and their gangs, with acres of remote, low-lying marsh out of sight of any riding officers.

It is very probable that the customs men did not want to completely stamp out smuggling, as they depended on it to keep them in work

Small-scale smugglers were usually just given a fine of three times the value of the goods, but they could also have their vessels seized, sold or even broken up. If they could not pay the fine they went to the debtors' prison, while gangs of professional smugglers were generally tried by jury. These full-time smugglers were usually armed, and fights with customs officers would frequently break out, in which men were occasionally killed. They would sometimes even attack a gaol in order to release offenders who had been caught, and break into customs houses to retrieve their confiscated goods. These smugglers' boats were often heavily armed, enabling them to repel the Revenue boats, and this, combined with an intimate knowledge of the local waters, led to many an escape from capture. The smugglers sometimes paid the local smacksmen to retrieve their sunk goods.

Geneva or Hollands were the names given to gin, geneva coming from the Dutch word genever, *meaning a spirit flavoured with juniper berries*

In 1729 the Great Yarmouth collector reckoned that 49,000 ankers of brandy (roughly 180,000 gallons) were being brought in illegally on the Suffolk and Essex coasts each year. Tea was an ideal commodity for smuggling as it was light in weight and could be bought quite cheaply in France to be sold on for ten times the price in England. In 1750 it was reckoned that the amount of tea brought in illegally each year was three times that of the legal trade. It was William Pitt who brought that to an end by cutting the tax on tea from 125 per cent right down to 12.5 per cent, thus rendering it pointless to go to the bother of smuggling it. It was reform of the tax system that eventually brought about the decline of smuggling: when income tax was introduced it was no longer necessary to tax goods so heavily, and by 1850 over 1,200 items had been relieved of import duties, leaving only fifty or so with customs still applicable. The Excise department remained independent of the Customs Board until they were merged in 1909.

Customs and excise duties were the main source of income for the Treasury until the introduction of income tax in 1799

COLLECTING CUSTOMS DUTIES IN THE NINETEENTH CENTURY

The commander of a Revenue cutter was paid £50 per annum, with a bonus of £15 for every smuggler convicted. The mate was paid £25 a year, and the sailors £8 each, but in addition to this they all had a share of the seized goods. The *King's share* was half the value and the other half was divided among the ship's company. While we worry today about the complexity of law and bureaucracy around the collection of revenue, it is reassuring to know that it has always presented logistical problems. This gallop through the various ranks of customs men gives an idea of how they struggled to manage the system . . .

There were legal wharves and customs wharves, and a *cocket* and a *transire* were clearance documents.

The revenue officer had a *hanger*, a short sword, and a *tuck*, a long skewer-like blade fitting into a wooden scabbard rather like a sword-stick.

The *collector* and *comptroller* were the chief customs officers. Originally the comptroller was the more senior but this reversed later.

The *landing waiter* examined the imported goods under the supervision of the *landing surveyor.*

The *tide waiter* did the boarding and rummaging under the supervision of the *tide surveyor.*

The *coast waiter* was responsible for collecting duties in the coasting trade.

The *riding officers* patrolled the shore under the supervision of a superintendent.

The *coal meter* measured and weighed coal for the calculation of customs charges.

The *Preventive Waterguard* was formed in 1809 and operated two types of vessel:

revenue cutters, often referred to as sloops, cruisers or smacks, whose commander could board and seize suspected vessels;

small sailing or pulling boats worked by *boatmen* under the supervision of a *sitter.*

The Preventive Waterguard became the Coastguard in 1822, and static anchored *watch vessels* with patrolling small boats were used instead. These were worked by boatmen who were also required to patrol on foot, taking over some of the riding officers' duties – the riding officers themselves were then renamed the *Mounted Guard.*

Geoffrey Chaucer was Custom Comptroller of Wool in the Port of London

SMACKS, BARGES AND BAWLEYS

The Essex coast still has a tradition of sailing the old working boats of the past, although now they are restored and sailed for pleasure rather than fishing. Always eye-catching when spotted in harbour or lying on a mooring, it is the sheer beauty of their lines that is so arresting. A working boat is designed for its purpose – whether that be dredging for oysters, trawling for shrimps or deep-sea fishing – and for the local waters it will be sailed in. Thus a boat designed for sailing in the deep waters off the west coast of Scotland will be very different from the Essex boats designed to perform well among

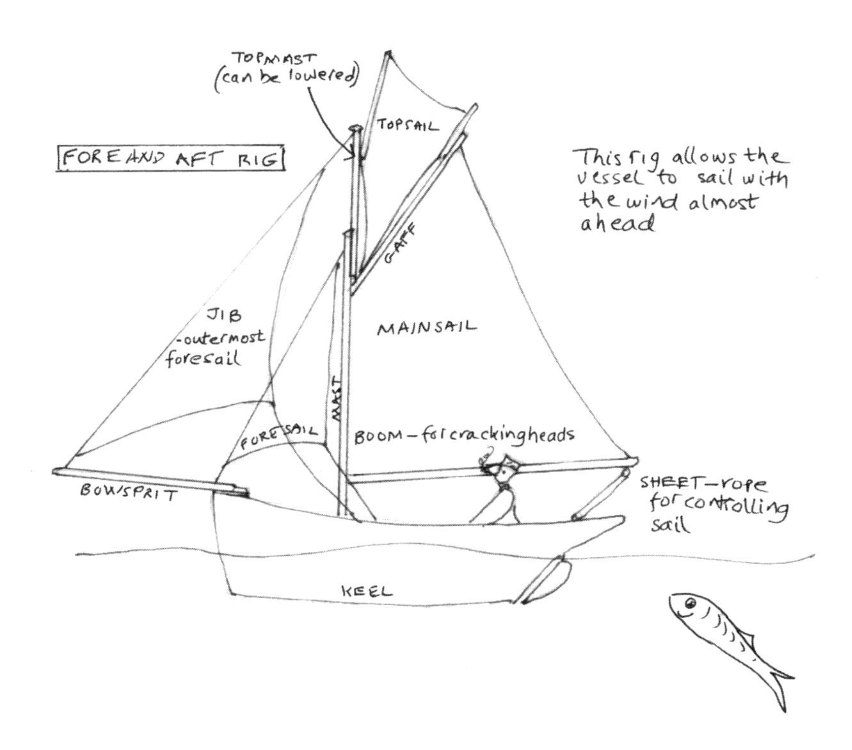

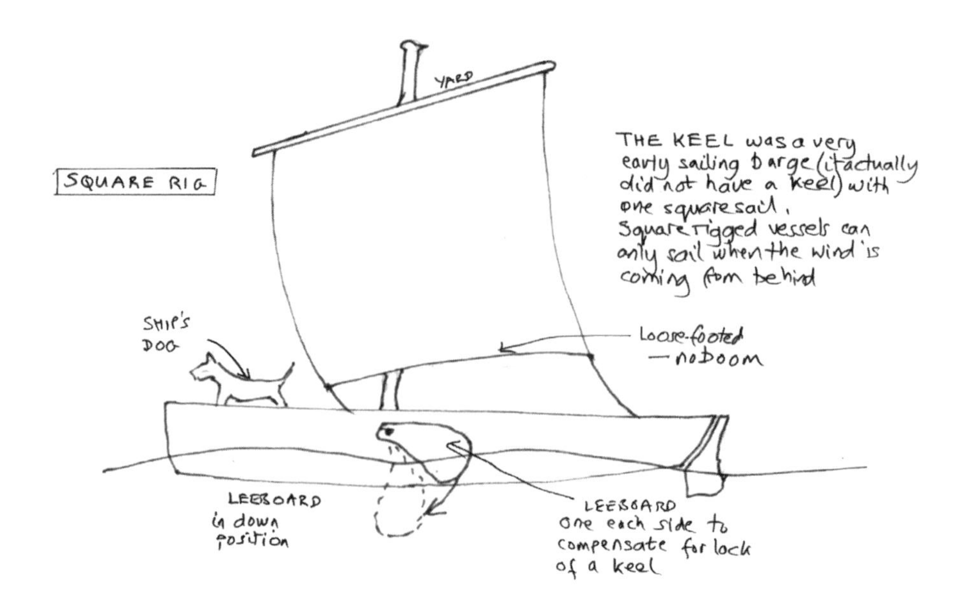

the sandbanks and shoals of the east coast. Except that 'design' is really the wrong word to use, as these boats were never designed on paper: they slowly evolved over time, built by men who knew the coast intimately and had an instinct for what would work. The result is not just a good working boat but also one which is pleasing to the eye, in that magical way that form and function are so inextricably linked. Nothing demonstrates this more clearly than a traditional sailing boat.

The term smack is a generic name for a working sailing boat, but there are many different types to be spotted around the coast. In 1894 all working boats were required to be registered, each boat being given a registration number which it had to carry on the mainsail. The number is composed of two letters followed by a number. The letters are a code for the port in which she is registered and are usually the first and last letter of the name of that port. Thus a smack registered in Maldon will carry the letters MN, one from

Lowestoft will have LT and so on. Vessels registered in Colchester carry the letters CK which stands for Colchester Creek, as there are other ports whose names also begin and end with C and R.

The **Essex oyster smacks** were of varying length, the smaller ones usually never venturing more than a few miles from home. The larger ones would be used for shrimping and stowboating for sprats, as well as dredging for oysters. Some were built for deeper sea work and went much further afield to the fishing grounds off the Dutch coast and north as far as Scotland. They had a counter stern which made more deck space available and a cutter rig; that is,

An Essex oyster smack

they carried two or more foresails on a long bowsprit. The **bawley** was a type of smack which developed in Leigh, on the Thames Estuary, and later also built in Brightlingsea and Harwich. Lacking the counter stern of the oyster smack, they were broader in the beam and had a loose-footed mainsail, which made working on deck safer when under sail, with no boom to sweep across the deck every time the boat tacked or gybed. They had the same cutter rig as the oyster smack and at first were fitted with a wet-well for keeping the catch alive. The bawleys used for shrimping would carry a copper boiler on board instead and this is possibly how they got their name.

The **Thames sailing barge** is the epitome of form and function. Evolving over the hundred years between the mid-nineteenth and mid-twentieth centuries, it became the most ubiquitous, the most beautiful and certainly the most versatile trading vessel ever to sail the east coast. Its peak came in the 1920s, but the years after the second world war were to see its decline as ships were needed to carry much larger cargoes. The small loading berths on the rivers serving the farmsteads of Essex and Suffolk were abandoned as farmers built bigger silos able to hold larger quantities of grain. Dutch motor coasters took over much of the coastal trade and the sailing barges had to be content with running short river-trips up to Colchester, Maldon and Ipswich. Some were converted into motor barges and many were simply abandoned to quietly rot away on the foreshore, but a few were kept on by enthusiasts for pleasure sailing and to continue the tradition of barge racing.

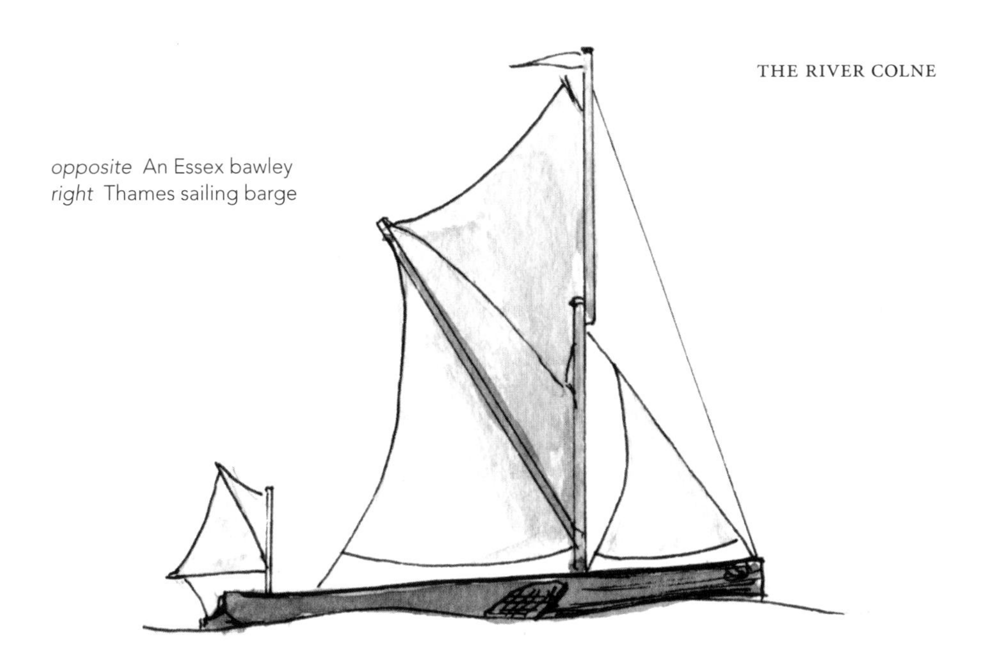

opposite An Essex bawley
right Thames sailing barge

Part of the secret to the success of the Thames sailing barge was its flat bottom, which enabled the barge to get up the shallow rivers and small creeks, and to sit comfortably on the mud at low tide, but it was also due to a sailing rig which allowed her to be handled by just two men and a boy. The large mainsail was held aloft with a sprit, a spar held diagonally across the sail from the foot of the mast to the outer corner of the mainsail, with a system of rope cradles, or *brails*, allowing it to be brailed up out of the way when not wanted, thus saving the hard physical work of hauling a large heavy sail up and down each time. The other sails, being smaller, could be handled more easily, and the whole collection of sails could be used in different combinations. The Thames sailing barge carried another spritsail on the mizzen mast which was usually sheeted to the head of the rudder. The lack of keel was compensated for by giving her a pair of *leeboards*, one on either side of the hull, which could be raised or lowered with a winch, depending on which tack she was sailing, to stop the wind driving the barge sideways.

The effect of all this was to make her into an efficient sailing machine at sea as well as being able to go up the creeks to serve small farmsteads, many of

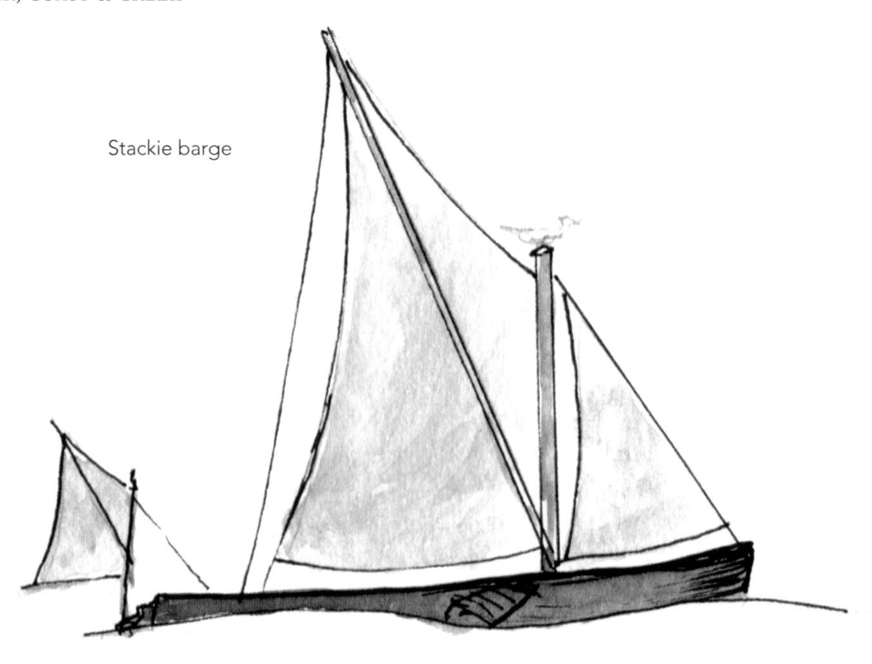
Stackie barge

which had only simple landing stages. A Thames sailing barge was generally around eighty feet long and fifteen feet wide. To give you an idea of scale, the mast would be made from a whole pine tree and the main horse – the spar spanning the deck, to which the mainsheet was attached – could be an old telegraph pole. Below decks, on a barge converted to pleasure sailing, there is plenty of room for several cabins for sleeping, and a large saloon with table and chairs to seat twelve people comfortably. There is still room for a piano, should you require one, and for a Rayburn in the galley. The hull is covered with pitch and you might find yourself being given a pot of lanolin and asked to rub it into the hemp rigging to keep the water out. The sails are stiff with their dressing of oil and red ochre and there is a pervasive smell of tar everywhere you go. Barge men are very fond of creosote. To stand on the deck of one of these vessels under full sail in a stiff breeze gives the feeling that you are standing inside a great engine. The sheer, raw power generated by the massive sails as the barge drives through the water is a thrilling experience.

The sailing barges grew in popularity as their abilities became apparent, and plough and sail developed a mutual dependency. Grain could be taken directly from the farm to the markets in London or delivered to the flour mills on the rivers. Manure from the London cabby horses was taken back to the farms, and **stackie barges** would actually have a haystack built on board, returning to London with fodder for the horses. The freight they carried was anything from brick-clay to linseed, sand, cement and stone. Barley was delivered to the maltings, and when beer was taken away it was customary to give the skipper a small cask for himself, thereby removing any temptation he might have to sample some of the cargo.

The flat bottom of the spritsail sailing barge gave it an advantage over the billyboy barges from further up the east coast. Those apple-bowed, round-bottomed barges which developed from the square-rigged keels on the Humber Estuary are pictured in many a painting from the East Anglian school. The workhorse of the north-east coast, the billyboy usually had a square topsail and carried leeboards on the hull. But the ability of the spritsail barge to handle well at sea meant she could also compete favourably with the collier brigs from the north, as well as the West country schooners which frequented the east coast.

In his seminal book on the subject, *Once Upon a Tide*, Hervey Benham uses the records of a barge named the *Arthur Relf* to demonstrate the sheer versatility of the spritsail barge. He notes that in her lifetime she took flour from Great Yarmouth to London, she went from Alderney with stone and took phosphates from Brittany to Exmouth. She worked for a while in the ballast trade on the London river during the first world war, took pitch from London to Dieppe and Calais, and had a spell laying cables in the Dover Straits. Coaster, river lighter, foreign-trader and cable-layer, all with no modifications needed to her cordage, rig or crew.

TYPES OF THAMES BARGE: THE TECHNICAL BIT

During the early evolution of the **spritsail** barge, the ubiquitous coastal trading ketch was modified to give her a flatter bottom and leeboards instead of a keel, but without changing her rig. The result of this variation was the **boomie**, or ketch, barge which was essentially a hybrid of the barge and the ketch. The boomie could navigate shallow water and although most eventually gave up their traditional square-rigged topsail, they largely retained the original ketch rig with its boomed mainsail and reefing points for reducing sail. Later on they were fitted with a tackle which could roll the sail around the boom to reduce its size instead: the roller reefing that is in common use today. The boomies were better at sea than the sailing barges as this ability to reef the sail meant the weight of the rig was brought much lower down, but they needed more men to crew them. Eventually, as the diesel engine replaced sail, it was the spritsail barge that outlasted the boomie.

A successful attempt to combine the best of the spritsail barge with the boomie barge resulted in the **mulie** barge. This was much like the spritsail barge but the mizzen sail had a gaff and boom and could set a topsail too. It was set forward of the wheel unlike on the spritsail barge where it was much smaller and set aft of the rudder post. The mainsail was smaller, too, which meant the sprit could be shorter, having the effect of bringing the weight further down, which again made her easier to manage at sea. A mulie barge usually had a wheelhouse added to give some protection to the person on the helm. Several of these were built with steel hulls in the 1920s, one of which, the *Thalatta*, is still working as an educational trust. Another, the *Will Everard*, lies in London's St Katherine's Dock.

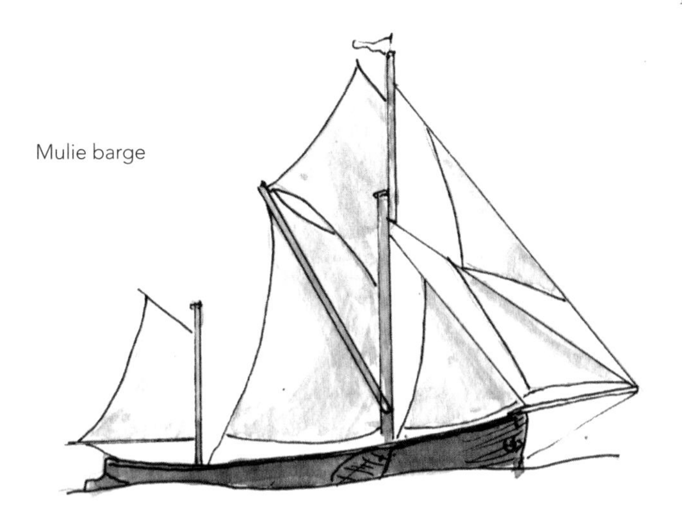

A number of Thames sailing barges went to Dunkirk in 1940. Some were lost on the beaches there or were bombed and never returned.

Dawn, built by Walter Cook of Maldon in 1894 as a stackie barge, was one of the Dunkirk Little Ships, and I was pleased to find her lying in the old Aldous yard at Brightlingsea when I was there researching for this book. A little smaller than many of the others and appearing to be more lightly built, she was a barge of the most graceful lines. I have a fine memory of her, one warm summer evening sitting on the deck of the barge *Raybel* as we lay at Maldon Hythe for the night. There was hardly a breath of wind and the water was still, as the afternoon turned into evening. It was a perfect end to the day as we watched *Dawn* sail slowly upriver towards us under her topsail alone with just her owner on board, bringing her up to the mooring under sail. It was fascinating to watch him adjust her speed every now and again by walking forward to one of the winches to lower a leeboard to act as a brake if she seemed to be moving too fast, and raising it again, equally casually, to allow her speed to pick up a little. She inched her way imperceptibly towards the quay and nudged gently into position alongside; a quiet demonstration of an age-old skill.

THE RIVER BLACKWATER

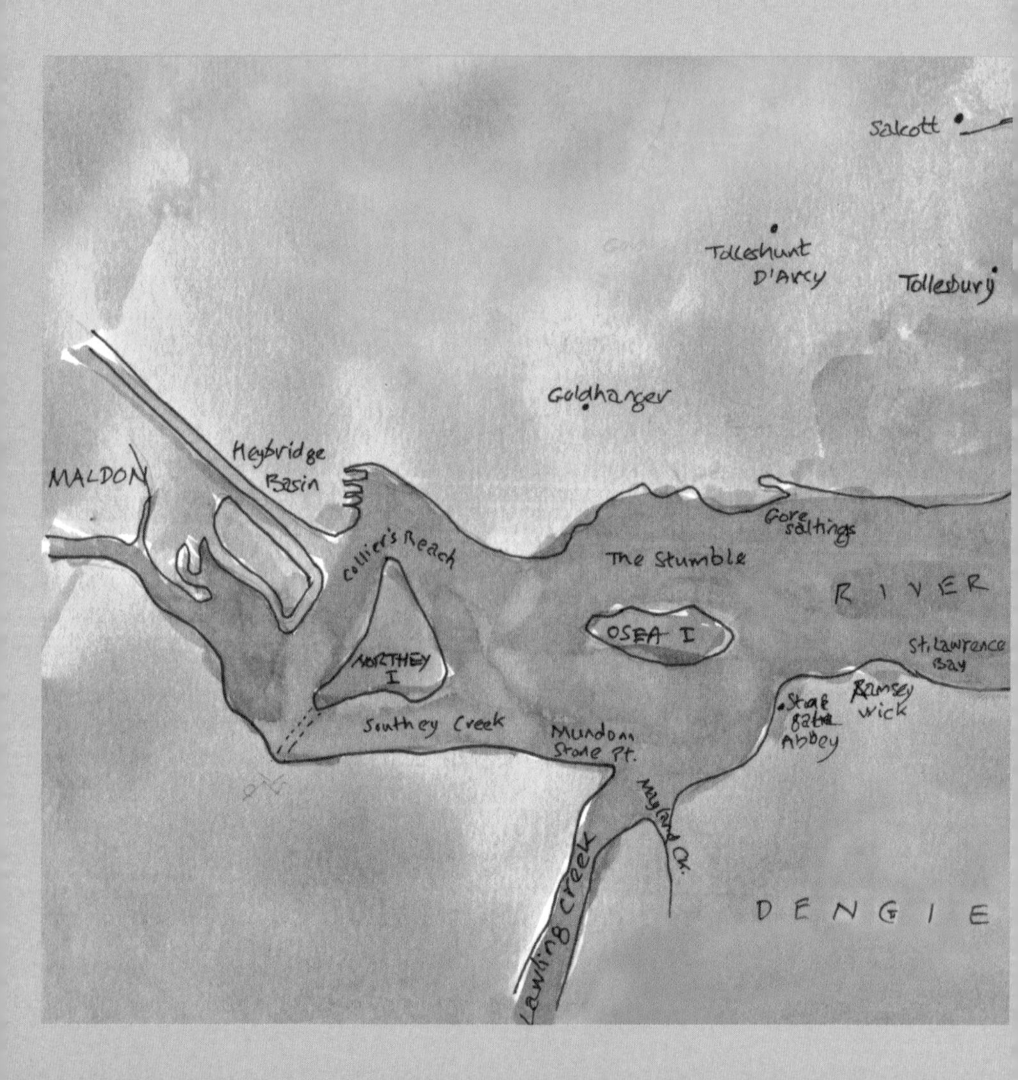

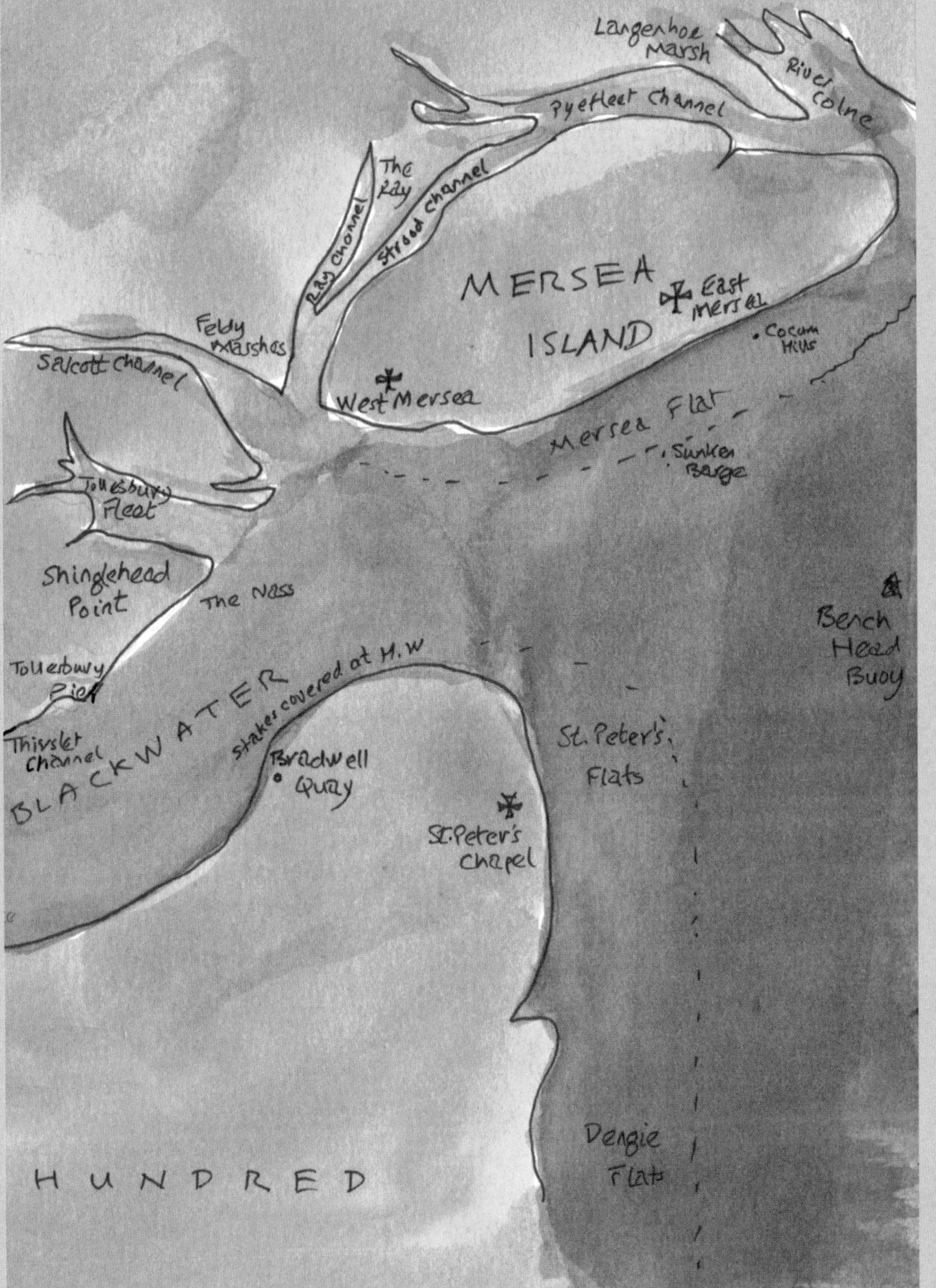

Langenhoe Marsh
River Colne
Pyefleet Channel
The Ray
Ray Channel
Strood Channel
MERSEA ISLAND
East Mersea
Cocum Hills
Feldy Marshes
Salcott Channel
West Mersea
Mersea Flat
Sunken Barge
Tollesbury Fleet
Shinglehead Point
The Nass
Bench Head Buoy
Tollesbury Pier
stakes covered at H.W
BLACKWATER
Thirslet Channel
Bradwell Quay
St. Peter's Flats
St. Peter's Chapel
Dengie Flats
HUNDRED

THE RIVER BLACKWATER

The river Blackwater was known in medieval times as the Pant. *Pant* is Welsh for valley, which may suggest that the origin of its name lies in the Celtic language of the early Britons here, the Trinovantes. The river opens out at Maldon into a wide estuary and if you should head out to sea from there you pass first Northey Island, scene of the great Battle of Maldon in the tenth century, and then Osea Island. The nautical chart offers the names The Stumble and The Barnacle to the water north and south of Osea, and a few minutes poring over the chart will reward you with more colourful names: Gore Saltings, Thirslet Spit, Pewet Island, and a little further out, Northwest Knoll, Bench End, Buxey Sand and The Wallet. How those names can ignite memories of days spent sailing among the shoals and sandbanks and channels of this beautiful part of the east coast.

As the estuary starts to widen out, Mersea Island nestles into the curve of the land behind, and across the water the River Colne comes down from Colchester passing through Wivenhoe, Rowhedge and Brightlingsea on its way. On a clear day the barn-like shape of St Peter's Chapel can be seen in its lonely stance on the edge of the Dengie Peninsula where it has stood for over 1,200 years.

Osea Island has been owned by noble families since the days of William the Conqueror, but in the early twentieth century it was bought by Frederick Charrington of the brewery company. Appalled by the effects of alcoholism on the children of poor families, he sold his share of the family firm and bought the island to set up a treatment centre for alcoholics. However, it proved all too easy for local people to deliver alcohol by boat and the clinic eventually had to close down. There is a story of a carter who used to bring in regular supplies of alcohol by horse and cart over the causeway. One day he was so drunk he fell off his cart and the horse plodded on to the island without him. The story does not relate what happened to the carter.

MALDON

The Romans made their first settlement at Heybridge a little further upstream from present day Maldon, but as the sea levels rose they were eventually forced to abandon it and the Maldon we know now is built on the higher ground overlooking the Blackwater Estuary. It was here that later on the Saxons, far more sensibly, established a *burh.* The *burh* was part of King Alfred's strategy for defence against the Danes; each *burh*, or town, was fortified by a wall and anyone could have land there in return for doing duty in its defence. They were often situated at strategic positions, particularly on rivers as the Vikings were very fond of bringing their longships up rivers to attack inland villages.

The town was granted a Royal Charter in 1171 by Henry II. In return for paying the Crown a regular tax and supplying a ship to the king when needed, it now had the rights to license its own fairs and markets as well as to raise its

Maldon's Admiralty Seal

own taxes. Many such charters were granted in the twelfth and thirteenth centuries, devolving a certain amount of power to a town in order to raise money, which was usually needed for whatever war the king was engaged in at the time.

The coat of arms of Maldon shows the three Plantagenet lions of the King and a ship.

Lying at the head of its beautiful estuary, Maldon grew substantially as a port, supporting all the associated trades of shipbuilding, rope and sail-making. It was the main port for Chelmsford, lying further upriver, and in medieval times many a load of wool must have come this way to be exported through Maldon, with trade expanding by the sixteenth century into both coal and the chalk needed for mortar and liming the fields. Growing in importance, the town was granted the right to hold its own Admiralty courts in 1528.

When the Heybridge to Chelmsford canal was constructed in 1780 most shipping bypassed Maldon and went straight to Heybridge. Some coastal sloops though continued to use Maldon despite the shallowness of the water, and barges would still come up to go under the bridge to Beeleigh Mill.

Samuel Pepys commands a naval ship

One of the ships built in Maldon, in 1654, was the forty-gun naval frigate the *Jersey.* She is remembered now through her connection with the great diarist of the time, Samuel Pepys. Never a member of the Royal Navy, in

1669 Pepys was temporarily appointed Commander of the *Jersey* in order for him to qualify to sit at a court martial pertaining to the loss of another naval ship, the *Defiance,* and he refers to this in his diary with some amusement. After fighting in the Battle of Sole Bay off Southwold in 1672, the *Jersey* was captured by the French, who used her as a privateer, and she was eventually sunk in action against the British in 1694.

> *Pepys kept his diaries in the nine years between 1660 and 1669 and much of our memorable history occurred during this brief period: Charles II was restored to the throne in 1660, the plague struck again in 1665, the Great Fire of London happened in 1666 and the second Anglo-Dutch war was fought from 1665 to 1667*

Salt

The wide Blackwater estuary is relatively shallow and the evaporation from such a large surface area makes its water even saltier than the sea and so an ideal place for the manufacture of salt, which still continues to this day. Salt was an essential commodity for the preservation of food in the days before refrigeration and most coastal communities made it to a greater or lesser extent. It was for the protection of the salt trade-route from Lüneburg to Lübeck that in the twelfth century the league of Hansa merchants was first formed, later going on to dominate sea trade in the Baltic and North Sea for three hundred years. The salt trade was an important part of the medieval economy, and the wily Venetians managed to engineer control of it in the Mediterranean during the thirteenth century by the ruse of paying merchants to land their supplies in the port at Venice, thus building up a monopoly over its supply and hence the price. There have been whole books written about salt. Commonly made all along the coast, it was usually done by the simple method of evaporating seawater in shallow pans, and this essentially is what still happens in the salt factory in Maldon, which continues to produce the familiar flakes of sea salt exported all over the world.

The Romans sometimes paid their soldiers in salt, giving the origin of our word 'salary'

Cook's Bargeyard

By the late nineteenth century the coastal sailing barges had evolved into that peak of form, function and design, the Thames sailing barge.

Walter Cook was commissioned to build the sailing barge *Dawn* in 1894 and this was to be the beginning of many years spent building and repairing the sailing barges that were so well suited to the transport of goods from the smallest farm to London and all the ports in between.

In 1907 the Admiralty had brought out the design for the new Montague whaler, and Walter Cook built a hundred of these boats for the Royal Navy during the war years. The whaler was a clinker-built open boat, twenty-seven feet long, powered by two sails and five sets of oars. Double-ended – that is, pointed at both ends – it got its name from the open boats that were carried on the decks of the great sailing whalers, from where they would be launched to pursue any whale unfortunate enough to be spotted from the main ship.

After the end of the second world war the yard was very busy with repair work to barges that had suffered damage from being requisitioned, and more and more of them came to Cook's to have diesel engines fitted.

But as the wooden hulls became older many owners were reluctant to spend more money on keeping them going and some were bought for conversion to barge yachts. The first of these was the *Challenger* in 1937.

Walter Cook retired in 1946, passing the business on to his son, Clifford, and the yard continued to thrive with work from Sully's, which owned the barge *Hydrogen*, and the Leigh Building Company, which owned a fleet of ballast barges. Clifford eventually retired in 1976 and the yard was bought and sold twice before being taken on by Topsail Charters in 2001. It is now the centre for restoration of the few remaining barges.

The Fighting Temeraire *was a 98-gun ship of the line commanded by Sir Elias Harvey, who came from Chigwell and was later the MP for Maldon*

SAMUEL PEPYS (1633–1703)

Pepys studied at Cambridge and then joined the household of Edward Montague, later to become the Earl of Sandwich, who got him a position with the Navy Board as Clerk to the Acts for the King's Ships. Knowing nothing about either ships or the navy, his curiosity, intelligence and sheer capacity for hard work soon put this right and led him to become a highly useful person on the Board.

The Royal Navy at the time was not only inefficient but steeped in corruption as well, and after defeat in the second of the Anglo-Dutch wars in 1667, Pepys set about making improvements. First addressing the poor diet of the sailors, he made it mandatory for every man to have a daily ration of a gallon of beer, a pound of biscuit and quarter of a pound of salt beef, fish, butter or cheese.

The next issue he addressed was to introduce education in navigation and to this end he helped establish the Royal School of Mathematics at Christ's Hospital in 1673 for the training of forty boys a year in the skills of navigation for the Merchant and Royal Navies. In the same year he was promoted to the position of Chief Secretary to the Admiralty. The Royal Observatory at Greenwich was built in 1675 and Pepys introduced the first examinations for naval officers in maths and navigation, as well as setting standards for pursers and ship's surgeons.

This was the age of a scientific revolution.

BYRHTNOTH AND THE BATTLE OF MALDON

The old Anglo-Saxon poem 'The Battle of Maldon' records the heroic defence of Maldon by Byrhtnoth in 991 during the reign of Ethelred the Unready, the longest-reigning of the Anglo-Saxon kings

Byrhtnoth was a towering figure of a man, said to be six feet nine, with a great mane of grey hair by the time he confronted the Danes at Maldon at the age of 65. He was not only the *ealdorman* of Essex, but his authority extended as far as Northumbria and he was one of the country's most experienced generals and advisers to the young king Ethelred. It was when Byrhtnoth was in the north that news first reached him that Ipswich had been sacked by the Danes, who were occupying Northey Island at Maldon. Leaving immediately to return south, he and his retinue were entertained overnight at the Abbey of Ely, where they were feasted royally, after which Byrhtnoth granted the Abbey several estates as well as payment in gold to have his body buried at the Abbey should he die in battle.

It was the year 991 and there was a new type of Viking on the scene. The Vikings that King Alfred had faced a century before were farmers as well as warriors, indulging in profitable raids on nearby coasts and just as inclined to settle in farmland more congenial than that of home. But these new Vikings were an elite army instigated by King Harald Bluetooth. Based at a fort in Jomsberg at the mouth of the River Oder, they were highly trained professional mercenaries, loyal and disciplined warriors. It was these *Jomsvikings* that Byrhtnoth was to face at Maldon.

Led by Olaf Trygvasson, a fleet of ninety-three ships landed on the east coast and, after wreaking havoc in Ipswich, some of these ships sailed up the Blackwater towards Maldon. Northey Island is surrounded by mudflats with a causeway connecting it to the mainland at low tide. Islands such as this were favoured by the Vikings for their encampments as they offered safe mooring for their ships.

It was unfortunate that Byrhtnoth was not able to raise an army of the size he wanted, partly due to the available men being fatigued by relatively recent battle and the need in August for them to get the harvest in if their families were not to starve the following year. Nevertheless, when the two armies met and the Vikings asked for Danegeld to pay for peace, Byrhtnoth replied that the only tribute they could expect was the point and blade of a sword. With that the first Viking came onto the causeway and was struck down by the Saxons. It soon became clear that the Vikings were cornered and their leader called out asking if they could cross to have a fair fight on the mainland. In what was to be a fatal decision, Byrhtnoth granted the request and formed his troops into the traditional shieldwall. They fought for many hours until, first feigning retreat, the Danes then turned round and in a wedge formation managed to break through the wall of Saxon shields. Byrhtnoth, standing head and shoulders above his men with his head of flowing silver hair, was soon cut down. It was not long before the Saxons were in disarray and, although many fought on, the Vikings were victorious despite the loss of a great many of their men too.

Byrhtnoth's head had been cut off but his remains were taken to the Abbey at Ely, where he was buried with great ceremony, the monks putting a ball of wax in place of his missing head.

His grave was opened during work on Ely Cathedral in 1769 and his body cremated. The ashes were reinterred and a stone plaque commemorating him can be seen laid into the north wall of Bishop West's chapel at Ely Cathedral.

The beginning and end of the poem have been lost, but the 325 remaining lines are recognised by scholars to be a masterpiece.

THE ANGLO-SAXONS

In the centuries following the departure of the Romans – the given date of 410 is curiously precise – Britain came to be divided into a British west, forming part of the Celtic world, and an Anglo-Saxon east which formed part of the North Sea world. How this actually came about is rather unclear due to the lack of both written and archaeological evidence. It is a bit like trying to do a jigsaw puzzle where most of the pieces are missing, but two basic narratives can be made from what evidence does exist and both are probably partly true.

During the fifth century Germanic tribes were moving westwards into France but they were not welcome under the rule of the Frankish Emperor Clovis and so were forced to move on across the North Sea, arriving on the south and east coasts of Britain. With the Romans no longer imposing order on society it is not difficult to imagine different warlords fighting for land and power as, unable to maintain the Roman infrastructure, people gradually drifted away from the towns, and resumed a more rural-based life. Gildas, a monk writing in the sixth century, gives us no dates but paints a picture of Saxon invaders driving out the Britons, burning villages and putting people to the sword. This version of events is endorsed by Bede, who was writing three hundred years later, and he even goes so far as to suggest that so many Angles had come to our shores that very few remained in their own country. Another version of the story suggests that the North Sea coast of Britain had long been settled by Germanic and Belgic tribes and that by the time the Romans left there were not many indigenous Celts left in the east anyway; Britain had already become divided into a Celtic west and a Germanic east. Whatever actually happened, by the end of the sixth century Jutes, Angles, Frisians and Saxons had all become established in Britain and were moving westwards. They had become the Anglo-Saxons: the English.

In the sixth century the west of the country was having a Christian revival, with Petroc arriving in Cornwall and Columba in Ireland later going on to found the monastery at Iona. This was the beginning of a flowering of many more religious houses in Wales, Scotland and Cornwall.

Early Saxon Society

The Saxons were a farming people. Not ruled by a distant king and court, they were free men (*ceorls*) bound by bonds of loyalty to their clan and the land which they farmed – their kith and kin. The centre of their society was the communal hall ruled by a chief (the *ealdorman)* supported by *thegns*, who would pledge to defend life and land in return for hospitality and military service from the *ceorls* when needed. This was rule by consent, which was later to develop into the Witan, an early precursor of parliament, which had representation from leading citizens.

Historians tell us there were seven Saxon kingdoms in the seventh century: Northumbria, Mercia, East Anglia, Essex, Sussex, Kent and Wessex. But in reality many of these kingdoms had more than one king. There were 'greater kings' and 'lesser kings' in these days, with a great king (*Bretwalda*) exercising extended power over Anglo-Saxon kingdoms. Bede records the great kings as the following:

Aelle of Sussex, late 5th century
Caeawlin of Wessex, 560–592
Aethelbert of Kent, 560–616
Raedwald of East Anglia, 600–624
Edwin of Northumbria, 616–633
Oswald of Northumbria, 634–642
Oswy of Northumbria, 642–670

After Oswy, dominance passed in the eighth century from the Northumbrian kingdom to that of Mercia under Offa, famous for his Dyke, and a century after that it yet shifted again, this time to Wessex, with Winchester as its capital under Egbert.

POWER, FEAST AND TREASURE IN THE SAXON HALL

The Old English poem *Beowulf,* written probably sometime between the eighth and ninth centuries, is a rich source for studying how Saxon society functioned. For many years it was only read by historians until JRR Tolkein brought it to general attention as a work of great literary merit and there is now a beautiful translation of it by Seamus Heaney. One of the themes running through the poem is the frequent reference to gold and the giving and receiving of weapons. Treasure was integral to the authority of the king, and the poem gives us an insight into this political world of power.

There were four things of great importance to the retention of royal power and first among these was loyalty from his followers. A Saxon king lived his life among his warriors, who slept in his hall, fought for him, feasted with him and were ready to die for him. Their numbers included men seeking service to him from abroad, often those exiled from their own countries. These men came both for adventure and for the expectation of reward, and their loyalty was crucial to the king's power. Secondly, success was always linked to the giving of gifts of gold and the king held the source of treasure; he was the ring-giver. Thirdly, the poem tells us how great store is set by the giving and receiving of finely wrought weapons, which were valued as much for their significance as treasure, as for their use on the battlefield. Lastly, it was the constant vigilance needed to live under the threat of feud. Life was insecure in those days and to retain his power the king had always to be prepared to fight and to use the giving of gold to maintain the loyalty of his followers. But to give gold also means constantly having to acquire it and when a king lost his ability to succeed in feuds, or lost his desire to give gifts, there was always someone younger and fitter waiting to take his place. The life of a king was insecure and often short.

The threat from the North

It was towards the end of the eighth century that the east coast first began to be raided by bands of Vikings arriving in their longships, looting for treasure. The monastery at Lindisfarne was brutally sacked in 793 and Iona in 806. Many more were to follow until in 865 the 'great heathen army' arrived in East Anglia and systematically fought and then occupied Mercia, Northumberland and Wessex. It was in Wessex that the Saxons were to rally under Alfred, famously leading his guerilla warfare from the marshes of the Somerset Levels. Raising an army, Alfred marched his men eastwards, finally defeating the Dane, Guthrum, at the Battle of Edington in 878. The victorious Alfred had the wisdom to seek a peaceful settlement with Guthrum, establishing the Danelaw, the partition of Britain giving the Danes the right to rule over much of the east side of Britain in return for peace. Alfred then set about laying the foundations of our present society. He commissioned Latin texts to be translated into English so the common people could be educated and, importantly, understand the law. He created the infrastructure of fortified towns, *burhs*, with the streets laid out in a grid pattern, where men were given land in return for its military defence when needed. He also commissioned the writing of the *Anglo-Saxon Chronicle* to record the history of Britain from Roman times and which continues to provide much information on the period to this day. Alfred's vision was to unite England under one rule, but this dream was not to be realised until his grandson Athelstan, by the judicious use of battle and diplomacy, finally brought England together under his kingship.

Peace however was not to last long. Athelstan died in 978, exactly a hundred years after his grandfather won victory at Edington, and thirty-eight years of chaotic rule ensued under Ethelred the Unready, during which Ethelred's preferred policy of paying the Danes Danegeld to avoid attack, was to lead to England paying out vast amounts of gold in protection money to any enterprising raiding Dane. The hapless Ethelred got it wrong again when he reacted to yet another attack, this time by the colourfully-named

Svein Forkbeard. The king ordered the immediate slaughter of all the Danes in eastern England, which included Svein's sister, who resided in London. In fury, Svein returned with a bigger army and Ethelred was forced to scour the country again for even more treasure to appease him. Over the next ten years the Danes gained enough control to force Ethelred to flee to Normandy, where he wasted no time in marrying Emma, the daughter of a Norman duke, producing a son who would later come to be known as Edward the Confessor.

When Svein Forkbeard died in 1014, the Witan invited Ethelred to return on condition of 'good governance'; the balance of power between monarch and men was beginning to shift. But the Danes were not going to go away and in 1015 Svein's son Cnut brought an army of 20,000 men in 200 ships to launch a further attack. A year later Ethelred was dead and Cnut was crowned king in London. He sealed the succession by marrying Ethelred's widow, Emma, thereby uniting a Viking Empire which stretched from Wessex to the north of Norway.

Thus did the rule of the Saxons come to an end, and a new era was to start when the Normans invaded Britain half a century later. But that is another story.

Ethelred's name in old English translates as aethel, *noble, and* raed, *well advised. The appendage Unready is a rather good pun for a king whose reign was marked by poor decision-making. Crowned king at the age of twelve after his elder brother, Edward, was assassinated, and with many of the experienced advisers at the court gone, maybe he should be judged a little more kindly.*

MERSEA ISLAND

Nestling snugly into the coastline at the mouth of the Blackwater Estuary, the small island of Mersea is in many ways a microcosm of the Essex coast. A mere five miles long and two miles wide, with less than half of it above the twenty-five-foot contour, it is a marshy, misty place which seems to belong to the water as much as to the land.

The first settlers to come here were Bronze Age herdsmen, who grew a little grain, grazed their animals on the marsh and trapped fish in the waters. By 500 BC, Celts from northern Europe had arrived, bringing with them their iron-making skills. The new iron ploughs were much stronger than the old bronze ones and the population grew, farming, making implements and thatching their houses with reeds cut from the marshes. The sea level was lower in those days and Mersea was still part of the mainland. They made salt on the shore by lighting brushwood fires under shallow clay pots filled with seawater, the remains of which are still to be found as the small mounds of burnt earth containing pieces of soft red clay known as 'red hills'. When later the Romans came to occupy Mersea it was populated largely by Belgic Catevellani, the descendants of the Celts from Belgium.

The kings of the Catevellani made their capital by the river Colne and called it Camulodonum after their god, Camulos. Their most famous king was Cunobelin, Shakespeare's Cymbeline.

The seventh-century monk Cedd is thought to have built the first church on Mersea, predating the present one. Cedd, a bishop and a member of the famous Council of Whitby, had come from Lindisfarne to restore Christianity to the land of the East Saxons. He is best remembered now for building the remote chapel of St Peter-on-the-Wall at Bradwell, standing on the edge of the Dengie Peninsula.

Sea levels rose after the Romans left, and the causeway which connects Mersea to the mainland is flooded for a brief hour at each high tide, a perennial reminder of Mersea's island nature.

When a new water main to the island was being constructed in 1978, workmen discovered the remains of some old piling lying under the Strood. It was dated to the seventh century and was at the time the oldest causeway ever to have been found in Britain. It would have been a costly structure

The old part of West Mersea is known as The City

to build then, both in materials and in labour, and the most likely person to have funded it is the Saxon king Sebbi, who later became Saint Sebbi.

A pious man, he would, according to Bede, prefer to spend his time in 'religious exercises, frequent prayer and acts of mercy', and would have abdicated the throne and entered a monastery if it were not for his marriage. It must have been the solitude and quietness of the island which attracted the king, and the causeway he constructed enabled Mersea and its lonely church to become a significant religious centre.

Excavations at Flag Fen, near Peterborough, have now found a causeway dating back to the Bronze Age

The Benedictine Priory at West Mersea

By the tenth century most of the West Mersea estates belonged to Ealdorman Aelfgar, but his daughters, Aelffaed (widow of Byrhtnoth, who we met earlier), and Aethelflaed (widow of King Edmund) left them in turn to the church. Subsequently taken over by the Crown in 1042, the estates were passed on by King Edward the Confessor to the Abbot of Omer, Normandy, who founded a small Benedictine priory here. The king then granted them a charter, giving them the rights to raise taxes from their lands. This was withdrawn however by Henry V in 1415, when he suppressed all alien religious houses in the land. He passed the properties of West Mersea, Peet and Fingringhoe on to Henry Chichele, the Archbishop of Canterbury. How casually it seems at this distance in time, that such large amounts of land and property could be commandeered and redistributed thus.

Nothing remains now of the priory.

East Mersea

The eastern half of the island is sparsely populated with only the occasional cluster of houses. This side of the island is all farmland and the roads mostly peter out on the wild salt marshes that edge this atmospheric place. Reeves Hall, a medieval manor house, stands alone amid its 750 acres at the end of a long track, like the handful of other remote farmhouses on the east side of the island.

The dedication of the church here to St Edmund-the-Martyr suggests that there may have been an earlier Saxon church on the same site. An East Anglian Saxon king, Edmund had been put to death by Vikings in 869 as they fought their way into occupying his lands. It was only a few years later, in 878, that the Danelaw in the east was settled under King Alfred. Edmund was shot through with arrows then decapitated, and legend has it that when his body was found, the head was missing. His supporters, hearing a wolf calling to them, followed the sound to find the wolf guarding the missing head. There is a beautiful modern carved wooden sculpture of St Edmund in the church.

The present church at East Mersea was built in the twelfth century using a wide range of locally available materials: you can find Roman bricks and tiles, boulder clay and flint in its walls. It apparently lies within a moated area enclosing about five acres of land, but I wonder why, in a place so intersected with creeks and waterways, that anyone would go to the trouble of digging a moat. Tucked away behind a wall at the end of a quiet road, the churchyard is a peaceful place now surrounded by trees with little to disturb its quiet presence. Four of its five bells were stolen many years ago and only the tenor bell, cast in 1492, remains. There is a story that the robbers who stole the bells took them to a small quay at the end of the lane to load them into their waiting boat, but the weight of the bells sank the boat and the bells now lie somewhere beneath the mud. No doubt there are stories of bells to be heard tolling from under the water at certain times of the year. I do hope so.

The Reverend Sabine Baring-Gould – the name may be familiar to churchgoers as the writer of hymns such as 'Onward, Christian Soldiers' – was rector here from 1871 to 1881. His withering remarks on the people, the climate and the landscape suggest he did not relish his time here very much. He did however write *Melalah*, the locally famous gothic novel set on the island. In the story the fiercely independent heroine, Melalah, suffers a lifetime of persecution from her cruel landlord, Elijah Rebow, who has become obsessed by her beauty. There are some beautifully written descriptions of the landscape among the rather quaint elaborate prose, and it is a rattling good story.

The name Mersea Stone can be seen on the Ordnance Survey map, indicating a point just off the easternmost tip of Mersea Island. It marks all that remains now of the triangular shaped blockhouse that was built as a defensive fort in 1543 by Henry VIII, ever wary of potential invasion on the east coast. Some years later Elizabeth I armed it in preparation for a Spanish invasion. It never saw battle, but its finest hour was to come in 1648 during the Civil War, when some Royalists were trapped in Colchester and the Parliamentarians used it as a lookout for the Royalist ships sailing up the Colne to rescue them. The Parliamentarians concealed their fleet in Brightlingsea Creek and were able to take the invading boats by surprise.

The bells of West Mersea church chime the tune of Sabine Baring-Gould's hymn 'Now the Day Is Over'

opposite St Edmund with the wolf

right There is said to be a mass dial scratched on the south wall of St Edmund King & Martyr, but I was not able to find it. Here is one instead from the church at Burnham-on-Crouch.

OYSTER FISHING

Oysters have been cultivated since at least Roman times and the harvesting of oysters has always gone hand in hand with their farming, as the oystermen in the summer months would bring the mature brood oysters into sheltered creeks to breed. But the methods of fishing with a heavy trawl have always been rather brutal to the seabed. One of the earliest trawls was known as the wonderthon. A ten-foot-wide beam, weighted with stones, supported a net twenty feet long, which had a mesh so small that no fish could hope to escape. They were banned for inshore fishing in a court hearing as long ago as 1377.

The oyster beds in the Blackwater were well known on the east coast and smacks would come from as far as Whitstable to dredge here for oysters, taking brood stock back with them to put down in their own oyster layings. The London clay riverbeds of Essex meant cool water, which suited the native oyster very well and the industry flourished for many years.

There are two species of oyster which can be fished from these beds: the native *Ostrea edulis*, which likes cold deep water, and the Pacific *Crassostrea gigas* oyster, which was introduced in 1980, preferring the warmer waters of the intertidal zone. These are referred to rather familiarly among the locals as 'natives' and 'gigas' and they were once trawled up from the seabed on an epic scale. In the nineteenth century it was estimated that two hundred million oysters were sold each year in the London markets, most of them coming from the Essex rivers. It was a major source of income for these fishing communities and it was to protect such a valued resource that a group of oystermen came together to form what is still affectionately known as The Company.

The **Tollesbury and Mersea Native Oyster Fishery Company** was formed in 1876 to restore and regulate the oyster fishery in the Blackwater. Half the shares were reserved for oyster fishermen and the other half were available to the general public, but local people were always favoured. It is probably one of the oldest limited companies in England. The company acquired the fishing rights on the estuary and set the dates and times when fishing was allowed, appointing water bailiffs to police the system. It was managed by a committee of twelve men called the Jury, who drew up rotas for fishing, but over-harvesting, disease and pollution eventually took their toll on the oyster population.

In the freezing winter of 1963 the entire oyster population was very nearly lost, and then in 1980 a disease caused by the parasite *Bonomia oysteri* struck. This, combined with the toxic effects of the TBT antifouling paint that most of the boats were using then, caused yet another massive drop in the population. It was now that the Company needed to get to work before the fishery was entirely lost.

In 1984 a small group of local fishermen managed to get a majority shareholding in the Company and they set about to improve and protect the oyster beds. They spent the first four years cleaning the riverbed with harrows to remove weed and sediment before laying down shells and rock chippings, known as culch, to provide the smooth surface the oyster larvae, or spats, need to cling to. When the oysters were trawled up to be sorted on the dredging table on deck, the larger ones were removed to the quieter creeks which gave them the optimum conditions to grow, and the smaller ones were thrown back. This local initiative gained speed when the University of Essex became involved.

The **Essex Native Oyster Restoration Initiativ**e was started by the University of Essex in 2019. The first important step was for the rivers Blackwater, Colne, Crouch and Roach to be designated as a Marine Conservation Zone and this status was achieved in 2013.

Oysters play an important part in the marine ecosystem in several ways. They improve water quality by filtering out the nitrates and feeding on suspended organic matter in the water, and an oyster bed also makes a valuable nursery for many species of fish, supporting a much greater biodiversity than an unstructured habitat. The loss of so many oysters over the last hundred years has had far-reaching consequences for the marine environment that were not fully understood in the past.

The aim of the Initiative is to re-establish the native oysters, restoring their place in a stable ecosystem while maintaining the stocks at levels sustainable for fishing. Working with the oystermen, conservationists and government bodies, an area two kilometres square has been protected as the River Blackwater Restoration Box. Culch has been spread on the riverbed for the spats, and mature oysters are transferred to the box to breed. Oysters are also being experimentally bred in tanks at the university, and the spats released into the box.

The modern oyster fishery today washes the oysters in fresh water tanks for forty-eight hours and then treats them with ultraviolet light to kill any harmful bacteria on the shell

SPRATS, SHRIMPS AND STARFISH

A sprat is a member of the herring family and sprat fishing was an important part of the east coast fisherman's income. They were fished from November through to February in the shallow waters of the Swin and the Wallet, and off the Maplin Sands (see map on page 2). It was done by stowboating, a method of fishing going back to the Middle Ages. The stow net was a conical net, up to two hundred feet long, with a small gauge of about half an inch. Its wide mouth was held open by two heavy horizontal bars of squared wood which were called baulks, the lower one weighted with iron. A system of ropes from the baulks and from its pointed end allowed the net and its mouth to be controlled from the deck, much like a puppeteer controlling a marionette.

A sprat

The smack would anchor at either high or low tide and lower the net, suspending it underneath the hull. There was a line running from the pointed end of the net to a buoy which floated on the surface to mark its position and another line from there attached to the delightfully named tonking post on the stern.

An anchored boat will always swing round so the bow is facing the oncoming tide

The trick was to hold the mouth of the net closed while hauling in the catch to avoid spilling any fish. The weight of the gear made it backbreaking work to control and haul in the net and this limited the size which was practical to use, so stowboating was usually done from the smaller smacks. The fish were smoked or pickled and exported in large quantities to Scandinavia and eastern Europe.

Sardines and pilchards are local names for other small members of the herring family, and what is called a pilchard in one part of the country may be called a sardine somewhere else

Shrimps were very popular in the nineteenth century and they were mostly fished from The Wallet by boats from Leigh and Gravesend. The shrimps were caught with a trawl net which was dragged across the seabed. The mouth of the net had a weighted bar, or sometimes just a rope which scraped along the bottom, and was either held open by a vertical bar in the centre called a trimtram, or with an upper beam shaped like an archer's bow. The Colne fishermen favoured the different arrangement of a D-shaped trawl head on either side of the mouth instead, which supported another horizontal bar above the scraper bar, and they often used several small nets rather than one big one.

The shrimps were kept alive in a wet-well on board and sailed round to London. When the railway was built and the catch could be landed at Harwich for onward shipment to London by rail instead, the fishermen could not land them fast enough to keep up with demand. By this time, instead of keeping them alive in the well, someone had the bright idea of carrying a large copper boiler on board so the shrimps could be cooked immediately they were caught.

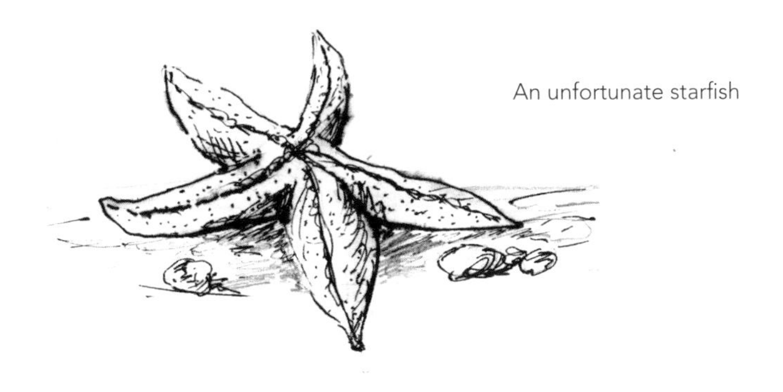

An unfortunate starfish

Starfish, known locally as 'five fingers', were fished specifically for spreading on the fields as a fertiliser. Such casual use of a living animal on such a large scale seems so wrong now, but this was also the fate of the sprat, if there was a glut and the price was not high enough. The starfish season was winter and early spring, but when chemical fertilisers became widely available there was no longer any need for the five fingers and they were left in peace.

THE RIVERS CROUCH AND ROACH

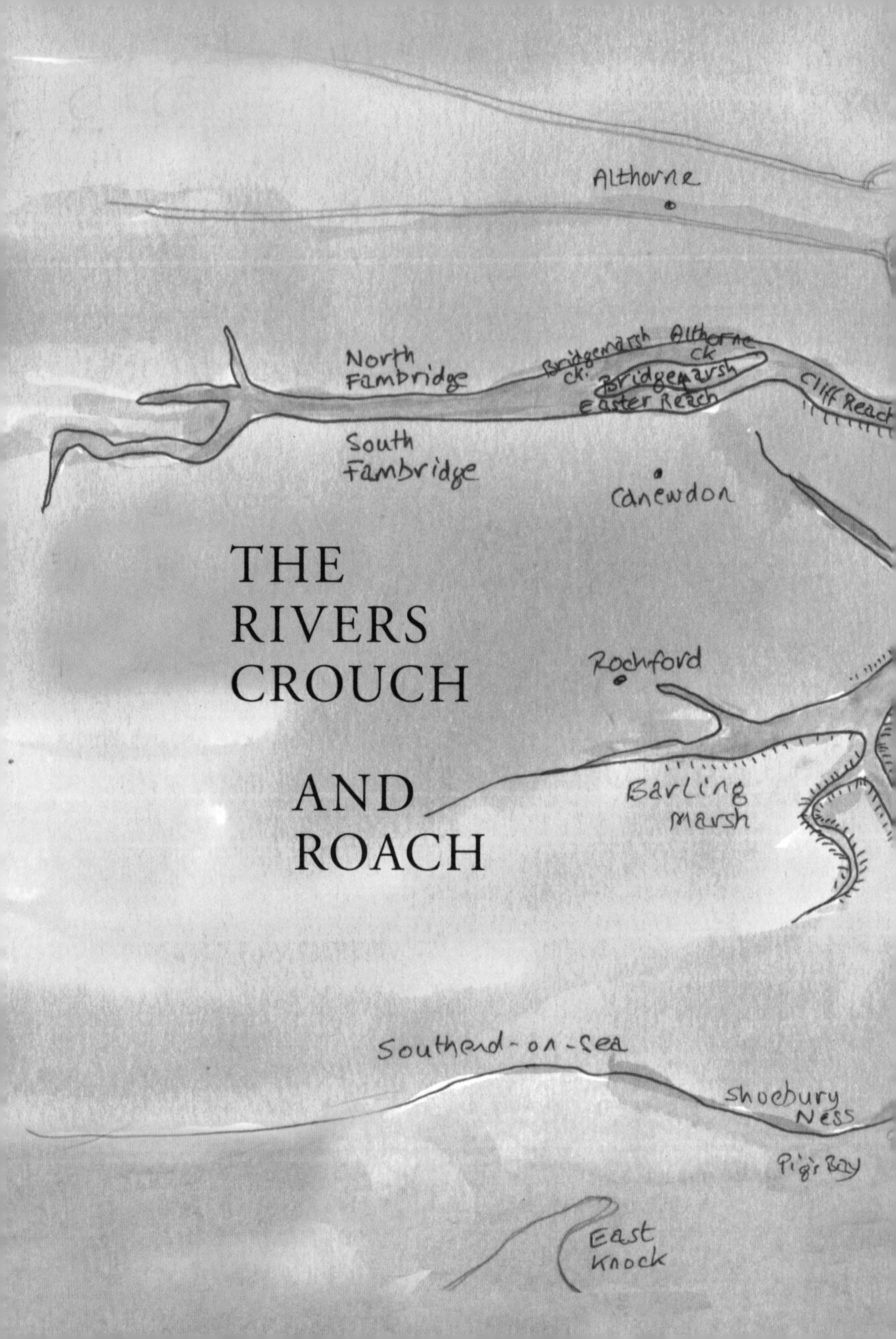

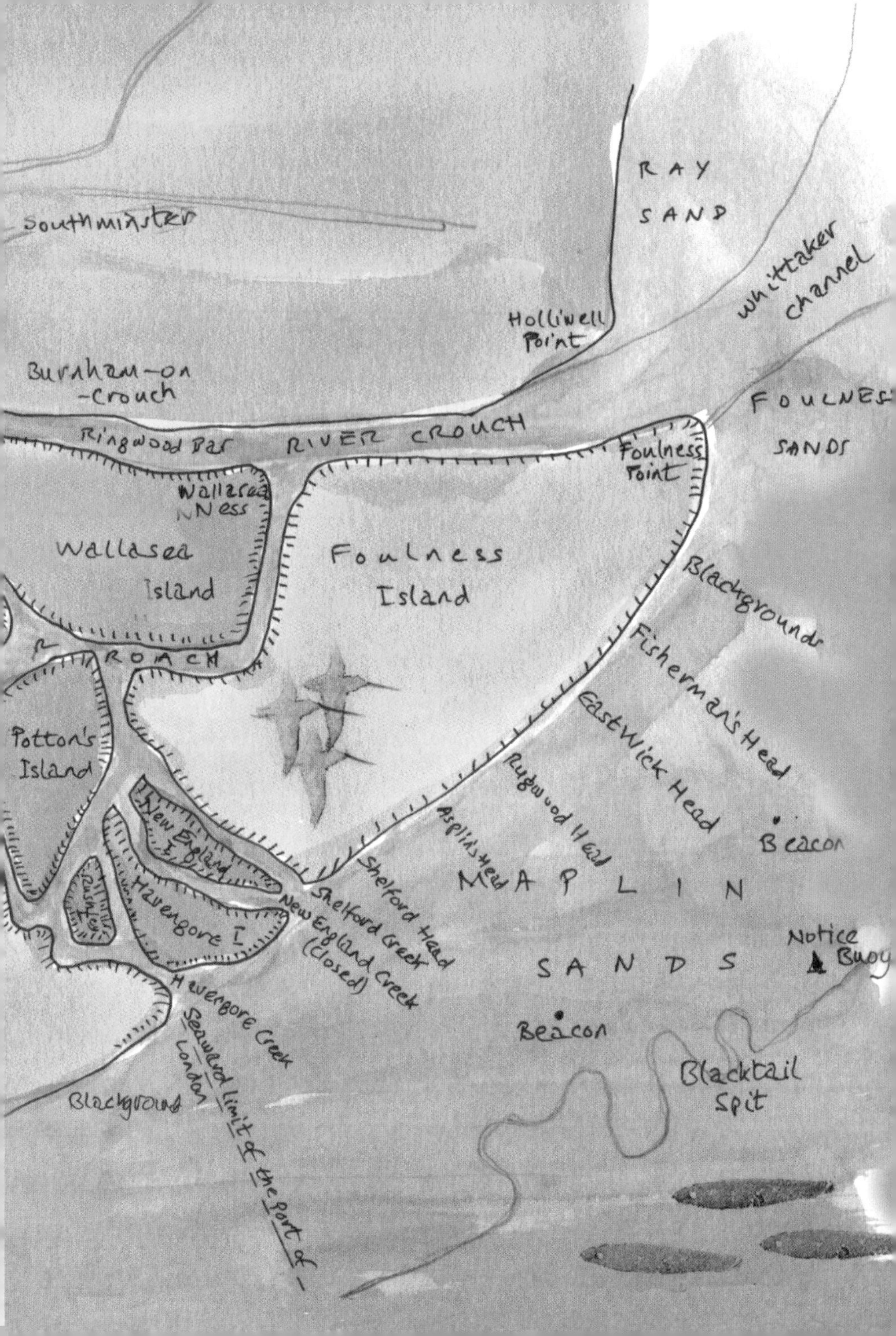

Southminster

RAY SAND

Whittaker channel

Holliwell Point

Burnham-on-Crouch

FOULNESS SANDS

Ringwood Bar

RIVER CROUCH

Foulness Point

Wallasea Ness

Wallasea Island

Foulness Island

Blackgrounds

R. ROACH

Fisherman's Head

East Wick Head

Potton's Island

Rugwood Head

Asplin's Head

Beacon

New England I

MAPLIN

Shelford Head

Shelford Creek

Rushley I

Havengore I

New England Creek (Closed)

Notice Buoy

SANDS

Havengore Creek

Beacon

Blacktail Spit

Seaward limit of the Port of London

Blackground

THE RIVER CROUCH

As you drive eastwards towards Burnham-on-Crouch, through the little village of Althorne, a glance to your right will reward you with a spectacular view over the river valley. A steel-blue arrow of water runs straight for most of its twenty-mile course. This is the river Crouch that rises near Battlesbridge and became famous for a while in the great days of yachting, when royalty and wealthy men raced their large, beautiful yachts from the Royal Corinthian Yacht Club. The boatbuilders and seafaring men of the Crouch and the Colne lived well on the economy that it generated. But for now the river from here looks peaceful and undisturbed, the reedbeds and mudflats quiet but for the wading birds.

Across the mouth of the river on the southward side lie the two islands of Wallasea and Foulness, except they hardly look like islands, more a peninsula of land divided by rivers and narrow creeks. It is as though someone has made a jigsaw puzzle of this part of coastal Essex and only loosely pieced it together again.

WALLASEA

Wallasea was reclaimed in the fifteenth century by Dutch settlers who built a seawall and farmed the land here, grazing sheep and growing crops. In the first and second world wars the rich agricultural land on Wallasea helped to feed the nation. Never densely populated, it is now in the process of turning back to an older period in its history. Parts of the seawall have been removed, and many tonnes of earth from London's Crossrail construction have been brought here to create a wetland nature reserve with mudflats, pools and salt-marsh once more, giving some natural defence from flooding on the Crouch as well as providing a habitat for birds.

Standing on the seawall here looking across this marsh on the very edge of Britain's east coast, it is easy to imagine oneself back in time to when early settlers first came to make a living from these wetlands alive with birds, fish and shellfish.

BURNHAM-ON-CROUCH

Burnham is a name familiar to all yacht-racing enthusiasts. The principal town in the Dengie Hundred, for centuries it got on quietly with its life, the river providing a livelihood for its people, who dredged for oysters, fished and built boats at the handful of boatyards, of which only one remains now. Burnham was put on the nautical map when the sport of yacht racing became popular in the nineteenth century. Many of the yachts designed for racing were built in the yards of the Colne and Blackwater, and both the Royal Corinthian and the Royal Burnham Yacht Clubs were established in Burnham at that time, providing venues for some of the races. Burnham Week is still a fixture in the sailing season, when for a week at the end of August, it plays host again to many competing yachts. Traditionally the races at Burnham were the last before the yachts were laid up for the winter for maintenance and repairs.

THE GREAT DAYS OF YACHT RACING

When the the Napoleonic Wars came to an end, many military and naval officers came out of the services with both time on their hands and income enough without needing to work. After the excitement of campaigning and fighting at sea, these men were not going to settle for a quiet life in the London clubs with a bit of shooting in the winter, and some of them were drawn to the sea and to sailing. This was the beginning of an age of competitive yacht racing that would enliven the economies of the boatbuilders and fishermen on the east coast for many years. The boatbuilders of the Colne had earned a reputation for building fast fishing smacks, so it was there that many of the yachts designed for racing were first built.

To sail these hazardous waters a fisherman needed a boat that was built to be fast. A boat with no engine caught on a lee shore (where the wind is driving the boat towards the shore) needs to have speed as well as manoeuvrability to be able to sail herself out of danger. This meant that the boatbuilders along this stretch of coast were experienced at building handy fast vessels. So when racing yachts were required, it was natural that some of these wealthy men would turn to the shipbuilders of the Colne and Blackwater for their boats and to the local seafaring men for their crews.

As yacht racing became established as a sport among the wealthy, the yachts became bigger, carrying huge amounts of sail, and rules were developed both for the races themselves and for the classification of the yachts. A rather confusing world now starts to appear as one reads of 'tonnage' (actually a measure of the volume of a ship's hull) and the 'International Rule' twelve-, nineteen- and twenty-three- metre yachts (when none of them actually were twelve, nineteen or twenty-three metres in length). Suffice to say that they were very big and carried vast amounts of sail. It must have been a thrilling sight to see *Valsheda*, *Shamrock* or *Britannia* under full sail offshore; we have just the old black-and-white photographs, some of which were made famous by Beken of Cowes, to go by now.

As the sport attracted more and more interest, yachts were being designed and built at yards all over the country and some of the names remain famous to this day, such as William Fife in Ayrshire and Camper and Nicholsons at Gosport, who built all the J Class yachts.

The regattas would take place all around the coast, from the Clyde and Aberdeen in the north to the Solent in the south, ending with a week at Burnham-on-Crouch, and they provided many fishermen with a good living, as they were employed as crew during the summer months when the fish were few.

This world has been written about by John Leather in his book *The Salty Shore*, where he tells that the daily wage for a hand in 1900 was one and sixpence, two and sixpence for a bowspritman, and five and sixpence for a mastheadman. Everyone had an additional half crown (two and sixpence) for each day's racing as well as one pound for each man if they won first prize, and sixteen shillings to each man for a second prize. It must have been such an incentive to the crew to work together and to work hard, but more than that, to know how much they were valued for their skills.

These days reached their peak in the years running up to the second world war, and although the America's Cup is still fiercely competed for, the days of those spectacular, beautiful wooden yachts and the whole era of skilled sailing men that went with them are gone.

THE AMERICA'S CUP

This was a trophy presented by the Royal Yacht Squadron in 1851 to the winner of a race round the Isle of Wight. It was won by a schooner called *America* and the trophy was renamed the America's Cup after her. It has been challenged for periodically ever since, in a race between just two contenders, the challenger and the defender, and over the years the rules under which it runs have been developed. It is a contest not just of racing skills but also of yacht design.

Britannia

From the late 1920s the Americans started to use their own universal rating rule, the J Class, rather than the International Rule and these mighty yachts were then always built with the America's Cup in sight.

One of the last J Class challenges took place in 1929, when Thomas Lipton challenged for the Cup with *Shamrock V*, built at Camper and Nicholson's yard at Gosport. She was towed across the Atlantic to meet the defending yacht *Enterprise*, owned by Harold Vanderbilt, and was soundly beaten in all seven races. Vanderbilt commented afterwards that 'the sportsmanship of Captain Heard and his crew is quite the finest it has ever been our good fortune to race against'. The captain and crew of each yacht sat down to dinner that night on opposite sides of the table, and Thomas Lipton died just two years later, aged 79.

Shamrock V was then sold on to Thomas Sopwith, who continued the tradition, later on commissioning the building of the J Class yacht *Endeavour II* at Gosport in 1936 in order to make another challenge. But she was to be out-sailed once more by Harold Vanderbilt in his even better designed yacht, *Ranger*. By this time the J Class yachts were becoming ridiculously expensive to build and sail, and the much smaller 12-metre yachts competed for the Cup instead.

This sketch is done from a photograph of the J Class yacht *Britannia*, which belonged to King Edward VII. It shows her under her full sail of 10,000 square feet. Built in 1893, she was 121 feet long and 164 feet to the top of the topmast. You can get an idea of her sheer scale by the size of the figure moving out along her bowsprit. He has his feet on the netting rigged underneath and there was room for quite a few more men to join him. As well as her foresail she is carrying an outer jib, called a yankee, and a large reaching staysail. The topsail is supported by two jackyards. Note also the graceful counter stern and elegant spoon bow.

ST PETER-ON-THE-WALL

Swathes of mallow and wild carrot edged the path leading to St Peter's Chapel as I walked the half mile or so out from the end of the road towards the sea. I was accompanied by dozens of young swallows wheeling and diving over the barley fields, practising their flying skills to the background music of a thousand bumblebees feasting on the wild flowers.

The chapel on the edge of the sea was built in 654 by St Cedd when he came to restore Christianity to the east coast. A plain barn-like structure, its walls are made of stone and Roman bricks, scavenged from the long-disappeared remains of the old Roman fort of Othona, which once stood here as part of the Saxon Shore defences. Restorations over the years have given it a fine tiled roof and a brick gable on the end that faces the sea. Sparrows chatter incessantly under the eaves, but it is not so much the building itself that makes such a moving impression as its setting within the landscape. This is the seaward end of the rectangular Dengie Peninsula, a promontory of land carved into a whale-like shape by the Blackwater Estuary on the north side and by the river Crouch to the south, and it is a flat expanse of land barely above sea level, margined by mud, marsh and sand. To the north the eye

travels across the water towards Mersea Island and the distant Naze, while to the east the North Sea stretches across to the Low Countries. But here there is nothing except the sound of the bees and the sparrows, and that enveloping sense of peace which often surrounds old monastic buildings.

The beach is made of thousands upon thousands of cockle shells, pounded by the sea into various grades of sand, a habitat known as cocklespit. The saltmarsh is grey-green with sea purslane shot through with the purple of sea lavender. Horned poppies lean their long seedpods to the wind and dream of the time when their delicate yellow flowers basked in the sun. Here is the place to remember the slow passing of the seasons and the chance to reset ourselves as just another small part of this wondrous, interconnected natural world.

The Saxon Shore was the name given to the line of defensive forts built by the Romans to defend the east coast of Britain from invasion by the Saxons

THE DENGIE PENINSULA

If the history of a city is written in its street names so is that of a rural landscape written in its place names. Looking at the Ordnance Survey map of the Dengie Hundred, these names caught my eye. What events and what people to they record? Now just an echo from a former time.

Squeak's House
Button's Hill
Twizzlefoot Bridge
Dammer Wick
Eve's Corner
Good Hares
Gunners Creek
Coney Hall

HUNDREDS, HIDES AND SHIRES

The Dengie Peninsula is marked on some maps as the Dengie Hundred. In Anglo-Saxon times the 'hundred' was a unit of local government and taxation. Consisting of one hundred 'hides', each hundred had its own court, which everyone could attend, usually held in the open air once a month. In the Danelaw lands it was called the 'wapentake'.

A hide was the land necessary to support one free peasant and his family. By the twelfth century it had become the amount of land considered enough to support four families.

Hundreds were subdivisions of shires, which were each administered by a reeve, the 'shire-reeve' giving us the word sheriff.

CARAUSIUS, THE FIRST EMPEROR OF BRITAIN

Carausius was one of the first Romans to hold the post of Count of the Saxon Shore and is thought to have been responsible for building most of the forts for its defence. The defensive line stretched from Brancaster in North Norfolk all the way round the east coast to Portchester in Hampshire, but the only signs left of the forts' existence are the remains which can still be seen at Brancaster (*Branodonum*), Burgh Castle near Great Yarmouth (*Garriannonum*) and Bradwell (*Othona*).

Coming from a Belgic tribe in the Low Countries, Carausius was a skilled sailor and, knowing the waters well, he developed a good sideline in profiting from the frequent raids on the east coast by pirates. He would wait until they had stolen their booty before giving chase to confiscate the goods for himself. News of his swashbuckling behaviour eventually reached the ears of the Roman Emperor Diocletian who immediately ordered his arrest, but Carausius responded by declaring himself Emperor of Britain. He then had the audacity to issue coinage with his own image and proceeded to set about strengthening the coastal defences. This made it very difficult for Diocletian to get rid of him and instead he was forced into accepting an uneasy sort of equality. But it was not to last long as Carausius was killed by one of his own officers just six years later

THE RIVER ROACH

The Roach begins near Rochford and snakes its way towards the sea, encircling the jigsaw islands of Potton and Foulness as it nears the mouth of the Crouch. It takes only a glance at the map to show how remote and unpopulated these islands are. The roads are few in number and there is little access to the shores for the land-based explorer. Everything on this coast from Mersea Island down to the mouth of the Thames is for the seafarer and the wildlife alone.

A footpath from the little village of Paglesham will take the traveller to the seawall along the edge of Paglesham Creek just before it joins the Roach, which leads back into the village again. The rivers here are largely left alone, used only for leisure now where once they would have been busy with working boats and fishermen.

That same map will show the Maplin Sands along the seaward shore of Foulness Island. The only access to the island for centuries was along the Broomway, an ancient track marked by bundles of twigs buried upside down in the sand, getting its name from the the bundles' resemblance to besom brooms. The tide comes in fast over the flat sands, and the water flowing from the two adjacent rivers creates disturbing whirlpools. When a mist creeps across the sands it becomes very difficult to discern the direction of the shore. Many a person has drowned here.

The remote stretch of marsh from St Peter's down to Holliwell Point was much used by local smugglers, who would sink their contraband in wooden tubs for later retrieval.

HMS *BEAGLE*

The *Beagle* was a ten-ton naval brig, later converted to a barque by the addition of a mizzen mast. She was refitted for a naval survey of the South American coast under the command of Robert Fitzroy, who had her hull strengthened and her bottom clad with copper to prepare her for the long voyage. Fitzroy felt the need for a companion and wanted a naturalist for the role; Charles Darwin, a young man destined for a career in the church, was to fill that role. The five-year voyage from 1831 to 1836 took them to the shores of Patagonia and to the Galapagos Islands, and what Darwin learned in those years was to change the course of science.

She was eventually sold for use by the coastguard, anchored off the river Roach as a watch ship against smugglers. In 1870 she was sold once more, for £525, worth that sum just for the price of the copper on her bottom. The *Beagle* is thought to be buried somewhere in the mud in Paglesham Creek.

A brig has two masts and a barque has three

THE FLYING SERPENT FROM ESSEX

The abundance of edgeland in Essex, with its marshes, mudflats and mists, is ripe territory for tales of a supernatural nature. The story of the winged serpent is one such: it first appeared in a pamphlet published in 1669, of which there remains just one copy, held in the British Library.

In 1885 two Essex historians obtained permission to make a facsimile and had a number of copies printed, offering them for sale at one and sixpence each. The intriguing story behind the tale of the flying serpent has been researched by Alison Barnes, an expert on the Winstanley family (mentioned below).

The pamphlet, which is illustrated with woodcuts, describes how a winged dragon-like creature had been seen the year before, basking in the sun near a birchwood. It was described as eight or nine feet long with small wings, large penetrating eyes and sharp white teeth. News of the winged serpent spread throughout the county and despite more sightings and numerous attempts to kill it, the creature always managed to elude them. It lives on in folklore as the winged Essex serpent, still able to strike terror into the heart of anyone venturing out alone at night.

The pamphlet goes on to describe a number of other monstrous and venomous serpents which had been recorded in far-off lands, including one from Tripoli (which the author thought was in Asia), which had a mouth so wide it could swallow a man on horseback. But the most fearsome of all them all was the cockatrice, a heraldic beast with the head of a cockerel, the wings of a fowl and the tail of a dragon. Hatched from a serpent's egg, it could kill by its stare.

The pamphlet records the local legend of a cockatrice which had once terrorised the good people of Henham, a village near Saffron Walden, and was eventually slain by a knight wearing armour made of crystal glass. The knight's sword and a brass effigy of the cockatrice were placed in the church but were later apparently destroyed by Oliver Cromwell's men during the Reformation.

The author of the pamphlet is unnamed but was very probably William Winstanley, who wrote among other things a popular almanac under the name of Poor Robin. An Essex man, he was born near Saffron Walden and was well known as a conjuror of some skill who loved to play practical jokes and who clearly came from a talented family. His nephew Henry was an

A fearsome cockatrice

eccentric artist, inventor and designer, who had been asked to build the very first lighthouse on the notoriously dangerous Eddystone Rock that same year. When the two men got together they must have been quite a combination and between them they hatched a plan to make an animated model of a dragon to see if they could scare the locals. They built the dragon out of wood and canvas, painted it and persuaded someone to climb inside to animate it. The hoax had the required effect and the rumour soon began to spread that a fearsome but elusive winged beast had been sighted in Henham. The secret was tightly kept among family and friends and the two Winstanleys went on to produce the small publication titled *Strange News out of Essex or, The Winged Serpent.* Henry illustrated it with some woodcuts, and if you look carefully you can see in one of them that the sun has a smiley face, the dragon looks rather friendly and the men pursuing it seem to be laughing . . .

HENRY WINSTANLEY'S LIGHTHOUSE

The Eddystone reef lies submerged just a few feet beneath the sea, a little way off the coast at Plymouth, and over the centuries many ships had met their end and many lives had been lost on its treacherous rocks. Trinity House had been petitioned in 1639 by two men with a proposal to build a lighthouse on it, but they were refused permission on the grounds that such an enterprise would be impossible. However, thirty years later the subject was raised again and this time Trinity House approached Henry Winstanley to see whether he thought he could build one there.

Rising to the challenge, Henry produced a design which Bella Bathurst describes in her book *The Lighthouse Stevensons* as resembling a drawing by Heath Robinson. The octagonal brick base sported a tower with an elegant iron balcony, a domed cupola and a lantern containing sixty candles; for good measure the whole contraption was topped with an iron weather vane. The structure began to fail within the year, though: the mortar between the bricks never set properly and the keepers complained that the whole edifice shook in bad weather. Undaunted, Henry set about reinforcing the brick base by encasing it in stonework and girding it with metal bands. He increased the height of the tower to 120 feet, added another, larger balcony and a gilded bedchamber complete with chimney and closet. It was finished off with an effigy of two cranes, several Latin inscriptions and six ornamental candlesticks mounted on the outside. Local critics were heard to say that it looked like something from a Chinese mausoleum.

Henry Winstanley's lighthouse stood until 1703, when a great storm caused devastation all over the south of England. Henry was on the Eddystone at the time, inspecting the light, which that night could still be seen from the land above the huge seas and spray until it disappeared around midnight. In the morning there was nothing left of the tower except twelve iron foundation bars. Henry had drowned.

MERMAIDS

The idea that a creature could exist which is half fish and half human is an ancient one; the interface between sea and land, water and air, has always held a fascination for man. It is a place where two worlds meet. Water conceals the world lying beneath its surface. It is an essential element to all creatures who live on land and yet, when the waters of a gently flowing river become swollen with rain and break the confines of its banks, it floods, drowns and destroys. Water sustains life, but it also takes life. A tranquil sea can suddenly be whipped up into a maelstrom. An underwater earthquake can trigger a tsunami; first the sea recedes like a mighty ebbtide laying bare the seabed, before giving way to an unstoppable wall of water travelling at speed and overwhelming all in its path. Thus was Britain finally separated from mainland Europe 8,000 years ago, and the universal fables of ancient floods which appear throughout all cultures would have had their origins in such an event.

The dugong is a marine mammal found in the Indian and Pacific Oceans. The manatee is a mammal of rivers and coasts and is found along the east coasts of Florida and Brazil.

Some of the earliest depictions of creatures which can inhabit the worlds of both land and water, half fish and half human, are seen in the ancient stone carvings of bearded 'merman' gods from Mesopotamia. Later the Greeks had their tritons and tritonnesses attendant on the sea-god Poseidon and loved by the sculptors of the Renaissance, but they are not confined to Europe. The mermaid appears to be a universal phenomenon, with China, Japan, South East Asia, India, Africa and the Caribbean all having their own versions of mermaid stories. As man ventured out exploring the oceans, many a superstitious sailor would have returned with tales of mermaids after encountering creatures such as dugongs and manatees.

Two-tailed singing mermaid

The sirens are sometimes shown as half human, half fish, but Homer does not actually give us a description of them in the *Odyssey*, he just describes them as voices which enchant sailors with their song. They are only given form later when sirens begin to appear in art, first as half human and half bird. By the seventh century AD they are more commonly depicted as half human and half fish; the siren seems to have become the mermaid.

A mermaid bridges the space between land and sea: she is a creature of ambiguity. She can live and breathe underwater but can also inhabit land, while man can only breathe air and cannot live under the sea. Add to that the power of the mermaid to enchant men and there is a disaster waiting to happen, the makings of the many legends of men marrying mermaids only to lose their wives to the sea and sometimes their children too.

The mermaid is a bare-breasted, sexual being and has either one or two tails. The single-tailed mermaid offers us the dual interpretation of being a phallic symbol while at the same time concealing the genitalia. The single-tailed mermaid can arouse but she cannot satisfy, whereas two tails make for no such ambiguity.

The mirror and the comb, with which she is often depicted, represent the moon and the plectrum with which the siren plucks her lyre. Across many cultures the moon is female, the *yin,* and the lunar cycle is held to influence fertility, with its resonance in the menstrual cycle and the practice of sowing seeds while the moon is waxing.

In German and Norse mythology, the moon is male and the sun is female

MERMAID MYTHOLOGY

There is a common theme running through the many stories of men and mermaids, none of them ending well. They usually tell of a man who, becoming enraptured by a beautiful mermaid, steals her cap, without which she cannot return to the sea. The mermaid agrees to live with him and bear his children until one day she finds her hidden cap and is at last able to return to the sea where she belongs, sometimes taking her children with her. In some stories the man follows her back into the sea and is never seen again. The mermaid enchants and gives life, but also deals death.

The 'selkie', or seal-woman, is another version of the mermaid myth. Confined to Ireland, Scotland, Iceland and Scandinavia, the legends of the selkies are very similar to those of the mermaids. The selkie appears to be a seal which comes ashore, removing her skin to reveal a human form. If a man steals her sealskin she cannot return to the sea until it is found again. From the Orkneys to the Faroe Islands there are stories of selkie-wives finding their skins and escaping back to the sea, leaving their half-selkie children behind. One story relates how one such abandoned husband is out seal hunting when he kills the selkie-husband of his former wife and two of her selkie-children. In grief-stricken revenge she curses the island, saying that men will drown and fall from its cliffs until there are so many dead that they can link hands around the whole island. To this day deaths on the island are attributed to the selkie woman's curse.

The selkie, the siren and the seal are all said to sing. Seals are known to have a highly responsive auditory system and can recognise their pups by their individual cries. They vocalise both under the water and in the air. There have been occasional reports of seals heard to be 'singing'.

MAPS AND SEA MONSTERS

The study of maps is at once a history of the known geopolitical boundaries of the day and a history of man's perception of the world. Old maps provide a glimpse into time when vast areas of the globe were known only to the people who lived there and oceans were yet to be explored. It must have been the ultimate adventure to set sail for a voyage out of your known world. Who is not fascinated by old maps? The modern 'Google map' is a sadly dull affair compared with a landscape brought to life with colour and imagery, and a seascape that teems with ships and sea monsters. The very early maps are known as manuscript maps, and as well as providing valuable geographical information they were showpieces for the skills of the cartographer. They were usually commissioned, often made specifically for collectors, while the charts made for actual navigation tended to have less illustration. There were two types of map in medieval times: the mappa mundi, a map of the world, and the portolan, or nautical chart.

The mappa mundi in Hereford Cathedral , painted on vellum, dates from 1300 and is the largest medieval map in existence

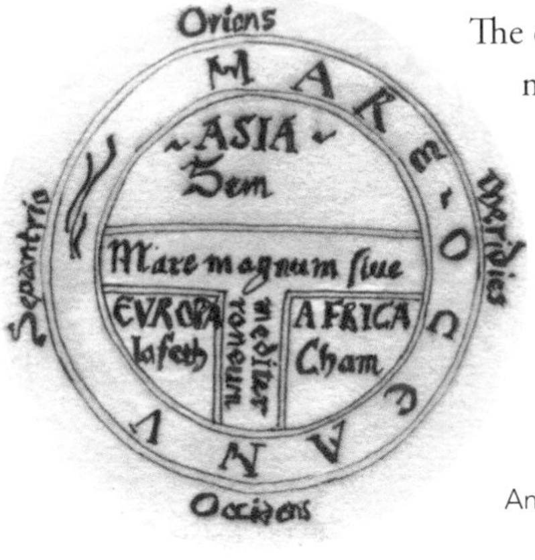

The earliest mappae mundi are called T-O maps. They showed the Mediterranean, the Nile and the Don (formerly known as the Tanais) rivers forming a T shape within a rectangular or circular border, making the O, which represented the sea. East was

An early T-O map

at the top, showing the importance of Jerusalem to the medieval Christian and Muslim world, and often had an accompanying image of the Garden of Eden.

> *The placing of east at the top of the map is the origin of our expression 'to orient'*

The earliest nautical charts surviving today date from the thirteenth century. They were not usually decorated, simply showing detail of the coastlines with their ports and towns, with radial lines criss-crossing the surface, each one peeling off from from the centre of one or more circles placed somewhere in the sea. These are rhumb lines and they were drawn in as a navigational aid for mariners plotting their compass direction.

The charts commissioned by wealthy collectors were much more elaborate affairs. The cartographer was often asked to add illustrations to the map, which allowed him to demonstrate his artistic skills and gave rise to wonderfully decorated maps adorned with images of strange beasts inhabiting the seas. These decorations had to be paid for, of course, and more money would buy you more monsters. It is easy to dismiss these images of sea monsters now as mere fantasy, but in fact most cartographers took the business of illustration very seriously and used the latest written texts and bestiaries of their day as source material; thus they were usually up-to-date depictions

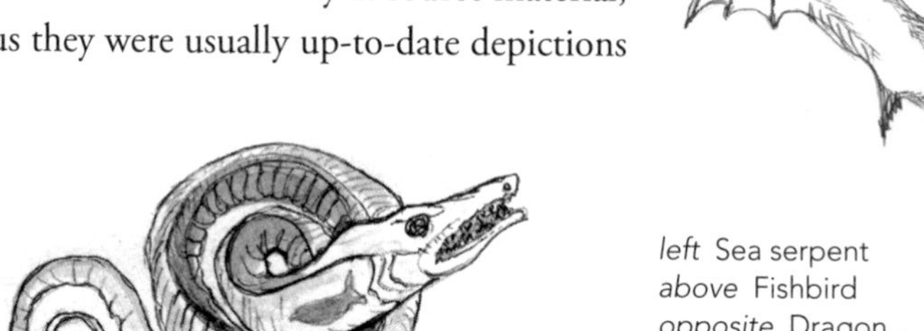

left Sea serpent
above Fishbird
opposite Dragon

of animals that were thought to actually exist. We may refer now to the extraordinary beasts depicted on the maps as sea monsters, but at the time they were produced they were considered to be accurate portrayals of real creatures and can often be traced back to the scientific works of the day.

The texts they referred to could range from the writings of Homer, with his descriptions in the *Odyssey* of Scylla and Charybdis, to the latest work of scholars describing the natural world. In much earlier times Pliny wrote in his *Natural History* that for every creature on the land there exists its equivalent under the sea that is fish from the navel down and animal from the navel up, and this idea coloured the way that man thought about the marine world for centuries.

Most marine life is concealed beneath the surface of the water and the underwater world of the ocean remains to this day the least-known part of the Earth, even with the highly advanced scientific instruments at our disposal now. How much more mysterious therefore for our ancestors, who relied on the stories of mariners who would come across whales and sharks of many different species and sizes, walruses, giant squid, dugongs and manatees. Stories which would no doubt have altered a little on every telling, as the best stories do, told of whales the size of mountains and giant octopuses grabbing sailors from the decks of ships.

St Brendan records mistaking a whale for an island and anchoring his ship on its back only to be wrecked later when the whale dived. There were other tales recorded of sailors even lighting fires on such a mistaken island, which disappeared under them as the whale plunged down into the depths. A whale could no doubt sink a ship simply by rising to the surface too close, but they were also reputed to be able to eat ships, and there are some pictures of whales with huge teeth and very impressive spikes coming out of their heads, actually devouring a ship. Although they were used principally for decoration, the pictures of terrifying monsters were often placed in the unexplored areas of the map, indicating the dangers to be found there, although this might also have had the effect of deterring future explorers. Apart from whale-based monsters, there were descriptions of giant octopuses, flying dragons and sea serpents hundreds of feet long, which could live on land as well as the sea.

The Renaissance saw a change in painting techniques, with the use of shading and perspective enabling much more dynamic imagery and this change can be seen on maps of the time as well. It was a time when classical imagery was becoming a new source for artists, and maps of the sixteenth century often use classical images of dolphins, sometimes with gods sitting astride them. Gerard Mercator's world map, first published in 1569 with his new projection, used the work of the French naturalist Pierre Belon as the basis for his illustrations. It is in the sixteenth century too that illustrations of whaling first start to appear, heralding the displacement of the sea monster from the map by the depiction of ships. By the seventeenth century, as the great European navigators continued to explore the oceans, whales were no longer portrayed as monsters devouring men, but as prey to be hunted; the prey had become the predator. Man had triumphed over monster and was now conquering the seas as well, taking the first steps on the journey which has led in our own time to our unwitting despoiling of the oceans.

Gustav I was the king who commissioned the ship Vasa, *now on display in a museum in Stockholm. The* Vasa *toppled over and sank shortly after her launching in 1628 and lay at the bottom of the harbour until she was finally brought to the surface in 1961. Her subsequent restoration pioneered the preservation techniques now used for other excavated ships such as the* Mary Rose.

THE MAP BY OLAUS MAGNUS

Olaus Magnus was born into a wealthy family in Sweden in 1490. His brother became Archbishop of Uppsala, and Olaus also held various ecclesiastical offices. He was well known at court and King Gustav I sent him to Rome on diplomatic business; he stayed on in Europe, brokering trade agreements and dealing with foreign affairs on behalf of the king. But while he was away Sweden embraced the Reformation and with those of the Catholic faith no longer welcome, he never returned to his native land. The Pope made him Archbishop of Uppsala on his brother's death, but it was merely a title by then and Olaus spent the end of his life in the monastery of St Birgita in Rome. He is mostly remembered now for his work *A Description of the Northern Peoples*, a book published in 1539 which described the wild seas and dark winters of the north, along with many aspects of life in Sweden from food to folklore, as well as descriptions of the animals to be found there. The lives and curious customs of the Swedes caused such astonishment in Italy to those used to living among the warm, vineyard-clad hills and olive groves, that it went on to be translated into many other European languages. The book also contained a map, the *carta marina*, which included illustrations of creatures to be found in the sea. One of these depicts a sea serpent, with the accompanying inscription announcing that it was two hundred feet long, twenty feet thick, and lived in the caves near Bergen, from where it would emerge to devour calves, sheep and pigs, sometimes even snatching sailors from their ships too. In an interesting parallel with present-day protection of national fishing rights, it has been suggested that he may have been induced to put his monsters in the sea to dissuade foreign fishermen from entering Scandinavian waters.

CODA

Essex has shown me three faces, three parallel worlds, side by side and yet so far apart. The railway and the motorway are the first, hurling commuters incessantly to and from London, epitomising man's brutal intrusion into the natural world and cutting scars across its second face, which is one of woodland, rivers and gently rolling hills. You have to try a little harder to find the third face of Essex, for there are few roads to take you there, but your efforts will be rewarded, for it is in the solitude of mudflat and saltmarsh, where sea meets land in an undefined, ever-changing transition, that you will find the true soul of Essex.

While writing this book I have repeatedly returned to the elusive nature of a boundary, where one state of being dissolves into another. The coastline is an area where land and sea continually morph into one another, where mermaids are half human and half fish and where Doggerland is forever suspended between fact and imagination. Even water itself is in a transitional state, somewhere between ice and mist; and it is when a mist hangs over the marsh that one is transported into a kind of magic, where half-formed ideas and images flit briefly across one's vision. A liminal space where time ceases to exist and all things are possible. This is the Essex that will be ever with me.

The story of mankind has been one long story of unforeseen consequences. But now as we approach the tipping point where the global temperature will be reset, man is at last seeing the consequences of his unlimited growth. Catastrophic for the human race perhaps, but not for the Earth, which will find a new equilibrium without us. The land and the sea can revert to a new steady point where nature lives in balance once more, and whatever happens to us, I like to think that wild geese will still find marshes to graze, terns, seals and otters will thrive in the seas and rivers again, and the sun will go on rising over a new day. For whatever man leaves behind, it will remain a mysterious and astonishingly beautiful world.

Reading list

River Colne Shipbuilders by John Collins and James Dodds
Saltwater Village by Margaret Leather
The Salty Shore by John Leather
Skillingers of Brightlingsea by Sean O'Dell
Exploring Historical Essex by Robert Leader
Smuggling in Essex by Graham Smith
Once Upon a Tide by Hervey Benham
The Illustrated Guide to Thames Sailing Barges by Rita Phillips and Peter Phillips
Sea Monsters on Medieval and Renaissance Maps by Chet Van Duzer
The Anglo-Saxons edited by James Campbell
In Search of the Dark Ages by Michael Wood
The Incredible Human Journey by Alice Roberts
Vikings by Neil Oliver
A History of Ancient Britain by Neil Oliver
Time Song: Searching for Doggerland by Julia Blackburn
The Flying Serpent: Strange News Out of Essex by Alison Barnes
The Lighthouse Stevensons by Bella Bathurst

Acknowledgments

My thanks to Niki Medlik, whose design skills have raised the level of this book to more than just a piece of writing and a few sketches.

In the course of my journey through publishing I have met many people in the book trade, all stalwartly carrying on in the face of digital competition and financial pressures, always with enthusiasm and warmth. My thanks to all of you too.